Devotions Inspired by Life

Because even an Ice Cream Cake
can Teach Us a Lesson about Jesus

Lynne Modranski

Mansion Hill Press

ALSO BY LYNNE MODRANSKI

Devotions for Church Leaders and Small Groups
Dive In to a Life of Freedom
Quiet Times for Busy Moms
A Reflection of the Beauty of God

DEVOTIONS INSPIRED BY LIFE
© 2020 by Lynne Modranski
www.LynneModranski.com

Published by Mansion Hill Press
Steubenville, Ohio
www.MansionHillPress.com

Library of Congress Cataloging: 2020913732
ISBN: 978-1-953374-00-4

In memory of my grandmother,
Florence Edna Crossley Stanley Pyles

Without your prayers and your dedication to Christ
our family would not be what we are today.

You influenced my journey with Jesus more
in your short life
than you could have ever imagined.

Contents

A Note from Lynne

Perspective drives life. Two people look at the same old lamp; one puts it out for the garbage, the other sells it as an antique. Point of view makes all the difference.

My grandmother, to whose memory I dedicated this book, understood this phenomenon. She and grandpa both lived with the worst kinds of auto-immune diseases. Yet, until I reached my twenties, I didn't realize their severity. Though she had every right to complain, Grandma chose to be joyful. She always found a way to bring the conversation around to Christ.

I, too, tend to be a glass-half-full kind of person. My lens may appear rose-colored to some; however, the trait has allowed me to find Jesus-lessons in the most unusual places. Animals, children, family, and food are just a few of the things that have inspired the meditations you'll find when you turn the pages.

You'll probably know me a bit better by the time you finish this book, but more importantly, I pray you grow closer to Jesus and begin to see His teaching in the everyday happenstance.

When you find Jesus in the simple things, tell a friend. Some think a lesson from a blue jay or a car key silly. But if Christ revealed Himself in that moment, it's a lesson to share. If it touched you, it will touch another.

I hope my life lessons inspire and encourage you as much as they did me. May you discover your Savior as you seek His face and mediate on His works and mighty deeds.

Live blessed,

Lynne

I will consider all your works
and meditate on all your mighty deeds.
Psalm 77:12

More Than You Think I Am

Now to him who is able to do
immeasurably more than all we ask or imagine
Ephesians 3:20 (NIV)

As the heavens are higher than the earth,
so are my ways higher than your ways
and my thoughts than your thoughts.
Isaiah 55:9 (NIV)

God often uses songs to teach me truths. I'll find a tune stuck in my head, and every time I turn on the radio, those lyrics start playing. Recently I caught myself humming a tune by Danny Gokey. For days it rattled around my brain. It's called, "More Than You Think I Am." Here's the line that struck me:

Be still and trust my plan. I'm more than you think I am [i]

When I heard this song the first time, those two pieces of scripture at the top of this page flooded my soul. I know God is bigger, higher, stronger, kinder, more loving, more merciful – more everything! I believe my Sovereign Father can do anything. I've lived life with God in a box, and I don't want to make the Omnipotent fit into my own little perspective anymore.

Yet despite my view of a limitless Creator, God forged this song in my brain. At first I didn't understand the lesson. I already believed these words with all my heart. But I soon came to realize God is even more than I imagine!

My Heavenly Father reminded me the importance of always looking for the magnificence of the Holy Trinity. Even accepting God's ultimate authority with everything subject to His plan can become a "comfort zone," a place with walls made of my own understanding. How many, like me, become so confident in the Almighty and his limitlessness, we forget there is more?

As much as I've seen God create and do . . . there is more. As much as I've felt the saving love and grace of Jesus Christ . . . there is more. As much as I have experienced the beauty and majesty of the gift of the Holy Spirit . . . there is more.

God used Danny Gokey's song to remind me no matter how close I get to Him, no matter how wide the doors of my belief open, even when I allow every ounce of His greatness into my life, there will always be more. Until the day I sit at Jesus' feet in Heaven singing "Holy, Holy, Holy" with all the saints, finally able to look at the face of Abba, this truth remains. My Savior and my King will continually say, "You think this is great! You ain't seen nothin' yet. I'm More Than You Think I Am."

Lucky or Blessed

~~~~~~

[11] "But as for you who left the Lord,
who forgot about my holy mountain,
who worship the god Luck,
who hold religious feasts for the god Fate,
[12] I decide your fate, and I will punish you..."
Isaiah 65:11-12 (NCV)

Dairy Queen makes a wonderful ice cream cake. This year I bought one to celebrate my dad's birthday. My siblings and I, with our spouses, took Daddy out. We reserved the back room so it would be easier to visit, and Daddy sat with his back to the door. After dinner, I went to the waitstaff to get the cake. When I returned, I snapped the plastic cover off and started to set the cake in front of the guest of honor to surprise him.

I forgot one detail. Experience reminded me a moment too late the black plastic base is slippery, and as I approached my dad's back, the cake slid. I quickly tilted it the other way; however, I must have overcompensated because our dessert appeared doomed to go down my front. Another quick move and the cake turned upright. But only for a millisecond, because now we were certain it would slide down Daddy's back. After a couple more slick maneuvers, I saved the humans but lost the battle. My sister and I both reached for the toppling slab of ice cream; the decorated top was destined to decorate the floor. Much to our surprise the cake did one more 180 and landed upright with only a bit of icing missing and a minor bend in the supporting cardboard.

Everyone laughed so hard we couldn't talk. It was the worst

rendition of "Happy Birthday" we've ever sung! My siblings enjoyed sharing the play-by-play with Daddy since the entire scenario happened behind his back.

Later that night I posted on Twitter, "You know Jesus is watching over you when you drop your dad's birthday cake on the floor, and it lands right side up!"

I wonder how many read my post and thought, "She's just lucky." Maybe, but believe it or not, this is the second time I've had this happen. (I know what you're thinking, "How could you let that happen twice?!?") I honestly can't believe luck would allow two ice cream cakes to remain edible after a drop from more than three feet.

Do I believe if bad things happen Jesus isn't watching over me? Nope. Sometimes life happens, and the Creator of the Universe allows the sequence of events to occur without stepping in. Most of the time there's something I can learn in the mess, and often the mishap allows God to be glorified in another way.

Regardless, I don't believe in luck. Isaiah 65 warns against it. Whether God intervenes or not, I will worship Him and give Christ credit for every good thing. I want to glorify my Savior at every turn, even when the events seem silly. Giving Him glory when everything doesn't go as planned needs to be a part of my life, too. Even if the cake had fallen upside down, I would still praise Jesus, because I believe He's always keeping an eye on things. And I think this time in His watching, He had a hearty, boisterous laugh.

Buzzards, Blue Jays, Bullies and Bad Guys

[1] "Do not judge, or you too will be judged.
[2] For in the same way you judge others,
you will be judged, and with the measure you use,
it will be measured to you."
Matthew 7:1-2 (NIV)

Recently, I saw a red-tailed hawk on top of a pole. I drove by slowly, hoping to see it take off in majestic flight. A couple miles down the road, I noticed another large bird with wings spread wide in the wind. Straining to see, I wondered if it was another hawk or, better yet, an eagle. Those great American icons exist in our area, but they continue to elude me.

When I got a closer look, my heart sank a bit as I thought, "Just a buzzard." Almost immediately this conversation began in my mind:

"Really? Just a buzzard? It's a creation of God. You thought it was cool hanging on the breeze until you found out it was a buzzard."

Why do buzzards disappoint me? Maybe because I see them every day. Or perhaps their small heads compared to their body make them unattractive. Their scraggly feathers certainly don't help. Nor does the fact they always sit by the road scarfing dead carcasses.

I started thinking about which birds I "respect" and which I don't. I know what you're thinking, "They're just birds!" But truth be told, eagles, hawks, hummingbirds, and small songbirds bring me joy; while Canadian geese seem quite dirty, and blue jays are bullies. Every spring I eagerly await robins, and I love the pileated red-headed woodpeckers outside my house. But the brown woodpeckers bore me. I can't even tell you his name.

All these revelations begged the question, "Do I categorize people like I do buzzards?"

Don't get me wrong; age, race, handicap, and gender mean nothing to me. But as much as I hate to admit it; I judge people and birds similarly. For instance, I think less of people who look "scraggly." What's scraggly you ask . . . Scraggly requires a bath and a comb, not because of a hard day's work, but because of days of neglect. Hopefully I don't treat these folks badly; I try to smile and speak, but my opinion of them closely resembles my attitude toward the buzzard. It's not that I dislike a buzzard, but it's just not appealing to me. I'd rather see an eagle or a hawk.

When I come across a bully or see someone begging when they appear perfectly healthy, my attitude is just as bad. I have to remind myself God created each one in His image. Each time I forget that simple truth, I find myself judging.

That lonely buzzard taught me a lot about myself. He showed me how to appreciate everyone as a creation of the Almighty, even the "buzzards" of the world. He reminded me to see every scraggly individual as a beautiful image of my Savior. Raised to appreciate social graces, I can be polite in every situation; but I want my thoughts to line up with my actions. When I act kind, what goes on in my brain should be kind too. The Holy Spirit constantly remolds me. So the time will come when I don't even notice idiosyncrasies. Until then, I'll continue to treat others as Christ would treat them . . . and I'll never look at buzzards the same way again.

The Call of a Robin

~~~~~~~~~~~~~~~~~~~~

…and his sheep follow him because they know his voice.
John 10:1-6 (NIV)

One morning as I stepped out of the shower, I heard a wheezy whistling noise. At first I thought it might be my dog snoring, but as I followed the evenly paced, high pitched sound, I realized it came from just outside my bathroom window. There on the corner of the roof next door perched a little robin. When the red breasted bird opened his beak, I knew I'd found the source of the sound.

I love whistling back at birds, so after I listened to his lonely call a few times, I tried to mimic it. I sent him a short single pitched whistle. The pitch wasn't quite right, but it made him stop. He finally returned my call, so I changed my pitch just a bit and tried again. Sure enough, he stopped chirping and began to look around. After several tweets back and forth, and the poor bird looking all over trying to find me, I remembered I was supposed to be getting ready for church, not whistling at a bird!

As I dressed and went through my regular morning routine, I wondered if the little bird had lost his mother. Had that baby robin been more mature, he wouldn't have given my mimicking tweets the time of day. I missed his pitch, and a full-grown robin has more of a "song" in her call. He obviously wasn't old enough to be familiar with the true tweets from his kind.

It reminded me of John 10:1-6:

> *"… the sheep follow Him because they know His voice …*
> *they will never follow a stranger …*
> *because they don't recognize a stranger's voice."*

I thought about the times I feel like that little bird. Sometimes I'm so eager to hear Christ, I mistake other thoughts and feelings for His voice. I'm anxious to find Jesus. Sometimes I want protection, other times I'm simply looking for advice or encouragement. No matter what causes me to seek my Savior, I've discovered the more I get to know Him and the more often I wait until I'm certain it's definitely His voice I hear, the better my life becomes.

Perhaps you've answered the phone and had someone begin talking without identifying himself. It doesn't take long before his timber, tone, or something he says gives the clue you need. But this only works with a friend, someone you know well.

And as you may have guessed (or already have discovered in your own life), the same is true for Jesus' voice. Until we've talked with our Savior and listened for His response on a regular basis, we won't recognize Him when He calls, and much like my little bird friend, we'll be easily fooled when a stranger tries to imitate the Holy One.

As Christians, knowing our Savior's voice is paramount. We need to be a 1 Thessalonians 5:17 people, praying continually. Reading scripture will help us become accustomed to the things Jesus might say. It may take some time; and like my new robin friend, we may mistake another voice for His from time to time. However, as we grow, listen, and get closer to Christ, we'll soon recognize His voice and then, like the robin, we'll be able to fly free!

A Lesson I Learned from a Bat

❦❦❦❦❦❦❦

⁴ There are different kinds of gifts,
but the same Spirit distributes them.

. . .

⁷ Now to each one the manifestation of the Spirit
is given for the common good.
⁸ To one there is given
through the Spirit a message of wisdom,
to another a message of knowledge
by means of the same Spirit,
⁹ to another faith by the same Spirit,
to another gifts of healing by that one Spirit,
¹⁰ to another miraculous powers, to another prophecy,

. . .

¹¹ All these are the work of one and the same Spirit,
and he distributes them to each one, just as he determines.
1 Corinthians 12 (NIV)

My husband, Steve, seldom, if ever, travels without me; however, one summer, when my work schedule and limited finances kept me at home, he attended two conferences on his own. The first week went by without incident, but the second, presented a challenge.

I dropped Steve and another pastor at the airport on Tuesday morning. On Wednesday, the grandkids came over to spend the night. Shortly after they went to bed, my grandson called down the stairs, "Hada, there's a bird in the bedroom."

I went upstairs to check it out and found his sister already sound asleep. Josh told me the bird had flown into our unfinished bathroom. So I duct taped an old sheet over the opening. We'd take care of the critter in the morning.

After tucking Josh in, I went downstairs to finish working. Less than an hour later, our dog began making noise. I ventured back up the steps to find both grandchildren asleep and Holly, our miniature Schnauzer, barking at something flying around the room. Not a bird. A bat.

Now, bats don't frighten me; however, I also don't like them flying over my bed while I'm sleeping, so I tried to figure out a way to get the bat out of the room. Prayer seemed like my best line of defense since Steve normally handles this kind of dilemma. Finally, the bat disappeared, so I went to bed with the light on and lightly dozed while I kept vigilant.

The next night, the grandkids were gone, but the bat returned, this time downstairs. I opened the front door, turned off every light except the porch light and the one near the door, and I prayed. I truly believe God is big enough to have led that bat out the front door. I know, you're thinking of all the ways I could have gotten rid of the bat. I've heard every one, throw a towel, hit it with a tennis racket and more, but I chose to trust that God would remove this bat from my house.

Exhausted, praying and crying, I wanted deliverance. About 2 a.m. the thought crossed my mind to open the back door, but I dismissed it as crazy. If the bat won't go out the front door, why would he go out the back? Finally, I went into the bathroom, the only room too small for the bat to hide, and cried some angry tears. I know for a fact God could have taken that bat out of my house had He chosen to, and to be perfectly honest with you, I was annoyed He hadn't!

The next afternoon my brother dropped by to help. Less than 10 minutes after he arrived the bat appeared. While he looked for something to trap the intruder, I opened the back door. Immediately, the bat flew into it. With the bat clinging to the outside of the door, I closed it. And just like that, he was gone. I'd cried and prayed over this bat for hours, and now in less than two minutes it was over.

My brother and I had a good laugh about my bat adventure. But later, when I prayed, I wasn't amused. Why didn't God answer my simple prayer on either of the two previous nights? Alone and afraid, I'd prayed, I'd believed, I'd expected. Yet I'd still had a bat!

In the midst of my angry cries, God spoke to my heart gently, "I haven't given you the gift of miracles, I've given you the gift of wisdom." And I remembered.

God had gifted me with the plan to get rid of the bat the night before. My back hall is about three feet wide with a low ceiling. When I opened the door, the bat had no where to go. If I'd have listened to my Father's voice when I first heard it, the bat would have been gone. But I had been tired, and I wanted a miracle.

God reminded me each of us have various gifts, and all can be used in the Kingdom of God. In this lesson from a bat, He showed me the importance of every gift for the body of Christ to function properly.

Some may seem to have prayers answered quickly and in full nearly every time they pray. Those probably have the gift of miracles. The gifts of prophecy, wisdom, and teaching can be intimidating because they appear so important. Tongues look like great proof of a person's spiritual health, but God said not everyone will have every gift. And while Paul told us to eagerly desire the greater gifts, those with the spiritual gifts of giving, works, hospitality and other less "showy" gifts should never feel inferior in the Kingdom of God.

The world sees pastors and teachers as indispensible, much like your hands and feet. We don't know what we'd do without these visible parts of our body. Yet, like your body without its liver and kidneys, when those less prominent gifts are missing, the body of Christ can not function.

If I had used the gift the Spirit gave me, I'd have had two good nights' sleep. And when each of us discovers our Spiritual gifts and uses them, not envying the gifts of another, we can be a powerful force, bringing others to meet the Giver of the greatest of gifts, Jesus Christ.

Lessons from an Egg Muffin

I eat egg muffins often, hoping they make for a healthier lunch than a burger. On one occasion the sandwich I received needed some serious help. The top muffin leaned to the left and the bottom to the right. The cheese hung half off the egg, and the Canadian bacon sagged on the other side. As you might imagine, my first thought dripped with sarcasm, "And they want to give the guy who put this together fifteen dollars an hour." My next thought was, "I hope whoever did this isn't a Christian."

As I arranged my muffin so it could be eaten, I remembered two verses:

> So whether you eat or drink or whatever you do,
> do it all for the glory of God.
> 1 Corinthians 10:31 (NIV)

> Whatever you do, work at it with all your heart,
> as working for the Lord, not for human masters…
> Colossians 3:23 (NIV)

I wondered, "Do Christians live these two verses? Do I live out Paul's words in all I do?" We're so immersed in this culture of mediocrity, even followers of Christ fall into the trap of a me-first mentality. When employers treat us badly, we often have a hard time working with all our heart. And if there's no personal benefit or it seems no one appreciates our hard work, doing it all for the glory of God becomes difficult.

But Paul didn't tell us to do these things when it was easy. He didn't say, "Whenever people are paying attention and the result could lead them to

Christ . . ." Nope, the apostle said, "whatever you do." And he said it in both verses. We may think some jobs too menial to perform in honor of our Creator, but a famous monk named Brother Lawrence peeled potatoes for the glory of God, and I have a friend who delivers mail as if delivering for Jesus.

Perhaps Christians should do an inventory each evening:

- Did I eat and drink to the glory of God today?
- Did I work as if Christ was my employer?

And if our answer isn't an emphatic yes, we'll need to make a few adjustments for the next day. Because while many have heard Colossians 3:23, fewer know the verse that follows:

> *. . . since you know that you will receive*
> *an inheritance from the Lord as a reward.*
> *It is the Lord Christ you are serving*
> *Colossians 3:24 (NIV)*

So whatever you do, do it for the glory of God today, as if you were working directly for Christ and not that human who pays your wages. Put those muffins together proudly, push your broom with joy, because Christ is preparing our inheritance. We may not get it today or tomorrow, but the day will come when the One who sees all we do, even in secret, will give us our reward.

The Breath of God

All Scripture is God-breathed
and is useful for teaching, rebuking, correcting and training in righteousness
2 Timothy 3:16 (NIV)

Once while chauffeuring an elderly friend with dementia and a weak heart, I took a turn a bit too fast. My passenger said, "You're gonna scare me to death." As we laughed, I thought, "Oh my goodness, I could scare you to death!" That's obviously something one doesn't say out loud, but it made me consider those common phrases we use every day.

We warn children their outrageous faces will stick, and every week at least one person tells me something costs an arm and a leg. We harass back seat drivers and tell actors to break a leg. Idioms, clichés, and exaggerations fly around so much I wonder how many people read the Bible as if it's one long figurative speech.

How would our spiritual eyes be opened if we took most Scripture literally? Even the figurative language and parables in God's Word reflect a more literal meaning than our flippant use of the phrase, "at a snail's pace" when we really mean, "Will you move faster?"

People reduce verses like Jeremiah 31:3, "I have loved you with an everlasting love," to broad, general terms. So few take that short phrase personally. We give Psalm 46:10 a quick read, "Be still, and know that I am God," seldom stopping for five minutes to reflect on God being God.

My life verse is Romans 8:28, "In all things God works for the good of those who love Him and are called according to His purpose." To keep it real, I've paraphrased it. This single verse gives me courage to step out on faith when I fear failure. I no longer need to beat myself up when I don't live up to my own expectations. I loosely translate it, "I cannot mess up anything so badly God can't make something good out of it as long as I am acting out of love for Him." I can quote it correctly, but my paraphrase allows me to make it my own. The verse becomes active and powerful in my life rather than just another catchy memory verse.

What about your favorite piece of scripture? Do you remember the reason it touched you? Does it still stir the same passion as the first time you read it?

My passenger's funny remark caused me to consider the way I read scripture. I want to be sure I'm not skimming or making assumptions about any Word my Father has spoken. I pray as we read His love letter, we'll remember that every line was inspired by the Creator and Master of the Universe. Every "dot and tittle" deserves our full attention because it is the very breath of God.

Perfect Peace

You will keep in perfect peace
those whose minds are steadfast,
because they trust in you.
Isaiah 26:3 (NIV)

And the peace of God,
which transcends all understanding,
will guard your hearts and your minds in Christ Jesus.
Philippians 4:7(NIV)

I've read the Bible from front to back almost every year since 1988, but for some reason in 2015 I felt as though I should double my efforts and read it through twice. I started strong, but after two and a half months life happened. My mother-in-law moved in and required a good bit of care. Despite the change in schedule, I kept pace to reach my goal, but only for one month.

In April, Mom broke a hip, and for several weeks, I spent every other night awake in the hospital making sure she didn't pull out any tubes. With only 8-10 hours of sleep every 48, my Bible reading plan went out the window. I read a chapter or two each day while sitting in the hospital; however, by the end of the first week, my brain could barely focus. I hoped I could make it through one time.

After a few weeks of beating myself up for falling behind, I realized my attitude was Pharisaical[1]. God wants relationship with me. He's not concerned

---

[1] *Pharisaical: Being like the Pharisees of Jesus' time. Following the manmade rules disregarding a relationship with Jesus.*

with the number of pages I turn every calendar year. So, I abandoned my goal. I planned to read at least a few verses every day regardless of my fatigue. Absorbing as much truth as possible became my new objective. I felt so blessed and loved in that decision.

In June Mom made it home. After getting settled in, I felt a nudge to resume my Bible reading plan. Just barely through the Old Testament, I couldn't see any way to get back on track to read through the entire book twice by the end of the year. But a few days of prayer convinced me this was God's idea, so I made a commitment to do my best. I put no pressure on myself, but Jesus cleared time for me, and I miraculously reached my goal.

The true miracle of this story is the way reading God's Word saved me. I am not a natural caregiver. When Mom moved in, I transitioned from a quiet uninterrupted work-from-home day to a schedule not my own. This drastic change forced me to live outside my element, and any other time it would have brought anxiety and depression. I faced neither. I believe God gave me a passion to read more Scripture so He could use His Word to keep my mind steadfast and give me peace beyond understanding.

I hope this short meditation encourages you to read your Bible as much as possible. Christ might not call you to read it through twice, or even once each year! However, I do believe reading at least a few verses every day transforms us. Whatever your scripture reading habits, if you need more peace, I encourage you to explore those pages so the "peace of God which goes beyond all understanding can guard your mind and heart."

Look Past the Pain

So we fix our eyes not on what is seen,
but on what is unseen,
since what is seen is temporary,
but what is unseen is eternal.
2 Corinthians 4:18 (NIV)

When my mother-in-law moved in with us in 2015, I felt blessed. My in-laws helped us so much in our first years of marriage. They supported us when we traveled with "Crossroads to Glory," and came to visit often when we lived out of town. So as mom began to lose herself to dementia, I felt honored to help her navigate her final days.

For a while.

Living with dementia can be difficult for the one who suffers as well as those who care for them. But my husband and I vowed we'd care for her in our home as long as we possibly could. However, a few weeks in, the magnitude of what we'd volunteered to do hit me.

Physically, my mother-in-law could run rings around others her age. Although her mind would be gone in a few years, her body could potentially last another twenty. As the realization sunk in, I came across that verse at the top of the page.

God reminded me to stay focused on Him. Focusing on the problem is much like looking at a rain covered window. If you concentrate on the droplets of water, you can't see beyond the pane; however, when you turn your eyes toward the beautiful scenery beyond the glass, a new world opens up.

Similarly, if we focus on the pain of our lives, that's all we can see. Hope vanishes as the source of our suffering becomes the only thing on our radar. The key to peace lies in turning our gaze toward Jesus. When we follow Paul's advice and fix our eyes on the unseen, those things that appear to be larger than life begin to blur. Like drops on a windowpane, our inner pain becomes barely noticeable when we adjust our lens.

When I focused on Christ rather than the ten years I might lose, I found joy. As I concentrated on getting closer to Him, I discovered peace. And though the time I spent caring for my mother-in-law ended up being only two years, the entire period became a time of spiritual growth and renewal because I learned to fix my eyes on the One I cannot see.

A Thousand Generations

Know therefore that the Lord your God is God;
he is the faithful God,
keeping his covenant of love to a thousand generations
of those who love him and keep his commandments.
Deuteronomy 7:9 (NIV)

Now and then I move into pity-party mode. When someone seems to fall off the face of the earth after I've invested a lot of time mentoring them, I start to wonder if my efforts impact anyone. If I let my thoughts linger there too long, discouragement sets in.

Recently, as I wondered if my witness made any difference, God showed me faint images of those I've been privileged to walk alongside on their faith journey. Soul after soul came to mind. Soon the figures became those of their children, faces of young people on track to live a life of abundance with Christ. God reminded me of Deuteronomy 7:9 and the "thousand generations."

This verse from Deuteronomy causes me to praise God that my faith gives my grandchildren and future generations a better chance of knowing Jesus. I thank Him for my grandparents and great grandparents who walked the path before me. Additionally, genealogy research has revealed martyrs and ancestors who came to America because they loved Jesus. Their lives made this verse even more special.

This verse and others like it give me hope for my immediate family. I cling to it as I pray for my grandchildren and future generations. God showed me the "thousand generations." His promise extends beyond my imagination.

Paul called Timothy his "true son in the faith." Likewise, those whom we've helped discover abundant life in Christ are our children. Every life we touch today may bring Christ's love to thousands of lives in the future.

That revelation encouraged me. I found hope for the times someone chooses to ignore my mentoring and fall back into their old life. Those seemingly wasted moments still hold the potential for a thousand generations of changed lives. Because one day each of those someones may recognize the grace I shared and choose to accept the covenant of love poured out by our faithful Savior.

Don't Build Your Own Fire

[10] *Who among you fears the Lord and obeys his servant?*
That person may walk in the dark and have no light.
Then let him trust in the Lord and yet depend on his God.
[11] *But instead, some of you want to light your own fires*
and make your own light.
So, go, walk in the light of your fires,
and trust your own light to guide you.
But this is what you will receive from me:
You will lie down in a place of pain.
Isaiah 50:10-11 (NCV)

Isaiah forces me to ask, "Do I light my own fires and brighten my own path?" Unfortunately sometimes I do. And while the days I follow Christ's light fall closer together than before, my strong, independent flesh prefers to take the lead and run ahead of God more often than I'd like to admit.

Human perspective wonders, "Why shouldn't I light my own fire? And do I really need God for something as basic as lighting a torch?" God revealed a truth to Isaiah; He wants to take care of every detail of our life.

So many times we march ahead on our own. I seldom think to consult my heavenly Father about dinner or my route to church. I don't need to bother a very busy omnipotent Creator with these mundane details. Do I?

Isaiah seems to think I do.

Years ago I began to let God light some of my fires. Getting on and off exit ramps challenges me. I like plenty of space between vehicles, so I started to pray for "holes" as I entered major roadways. And amazingly enough, now I never have to fight traffic. My answered highway prayers demonstrate God wants to take care of the most minute elements in my life.

Isaiah takes it a step further. When I choose to take care of the everyday things, light my own fires, without consulting my Heavenly Father first, I set myself up for pain. Our prayer time shouldn't become full of legalism, but to avoid the torment that Isaiah says comes from self-reliance, we need to submit to the Savior on the most basic level. We experience enough hardship courtesy of life. It's foolishness to pile on more because we refuse to trust God with the smallest detail.

So from this day forward I plan to give God the matches. He can take care of the fires. I want Him to light my way and make the final decision regarding my most minute plans. Because with God in charge, when I lie down, I can truly rest!

The Tyranny of the Urgent

Seek first the kingdom of God and His righteousness
and all these things will be given to you as well.
Matthew 6:33 (NIV)

So whether we are at home or away,
we make it our priority to please Him
2 Corinthians 5:9

A rainy cold spring kept me from power washing my deck until late June. Usually Steve would have helped, but the truck needed work, so he spent the entire day under the hood.

As I worked alone, I thought about a phrase I've heard many times, "The Tyranny of the Urgent." We set priorities, and our hearts understand what's truly important, but the urgent tears us away. Steve's truck was a perfect example.

Matthew 6:33 tells us seeking God must come before anything else. Sadly, the urgent speaks with a very insistent tone. For instance, our kids' sporting events overlap worship service. Some gadget breaks and robs our quiet time with Christ. Reading the Bible tops our to-do list until we find ourselves running late for work.

I've been blessed to have a Matthew 6:33 husband. Since the day he asked Christ to be his Savior, Steve's relationship with the Creator has been a priority. Even before becoming a pastor, he postponed sleep after midnight shift to attend worship. He's always carried a small Bible so when traffic comes to a halt or there's a lull in his day, he can dive into scripture. And this

Sunday, when his truck still needed work after that long afternoon with the engine, he went to church, preached God's word and spent the rest of the day relaxing, visiting with our daughters and watching the grandkids in the pool.

The tyranny of the urgent screamed, "Work on that truck!" But the Kingdom of God says, "I created the Sabbath for rest, and I made you for relationships." He spent an entire Sunday building his relationship with his Heavenly Father and two of our daughters. The urgent can wait on the important.

Granted, the urgent sometimes demands our attention. For instance, Steve nearly cut his finger off a couple months ago. The urgent won that day. We spent hours in an emergency room and had to reschedule our plans for a Toby Mac concert. On a side note, they saved his finger, and we were able to transfer our tickets to another venue.

Unfortunately, sometimes in our humanness, Steve and I needlessly give into the tyranny, missing opportunities Jesus puts in our path. Occasionally we see it and get back on track, but too often we let the tyranny win. The tyranny of the urgent causes a feeling of helplessness. It feeds us lies until we cater to its demand and neglect what's truly important.

However, when we remember to diligently and purposefully search for the Kingdom of God, we discover it's possible to make His plans our priority. Because many times the things Christ "adds to us" are wisdom, time, and freedom from the urgent.

Can You Take the Heat?

But blessed is the one who trusts in the LORD, . . .
⁸ They will be like a tree planted by the water . . .
It does not fear when heat comes; . . .
It has no worries in a year of drought . . ."
Jeremiah 17:7-8 (NIV)

The Bible mentions the "refiner's fire" at least four times. Isaiah 48:10 calls it the furnace of affliction. Zechariah 13:9 says we are refined like silver and gold so we can be called people of the Lord, and Daniel 11 talks about the wise being refined.

Fortunately, Jeremiah reminds us when we trust in the Lord, we don't need to fear the refiner's fire. When I gave my life to Christ, I read this verse wrong. I thought salvation meant my problems were over. I'm not sure where I got that idea. But Jeremiah doesn't say that those who trust are exempt from the fire. He says we won't fear when the heat comes.

My skewed view may have come from my wonderful grandmother. The godliest woman you've ever seen, she never came across as pious or sanctimonious. Grandma just blatantly loved Jesus. Sadly, she suffered from Lupus. The disease took her before my seventeenth birthday. She lost Grandpa to another deadly disease before he reached sixty, and they lived on a very meager income. Grandma's life epitomized a Christian with problems. Regardless, she never complained. Because she demonstrated the life of a "tree planted by the water" that "does not fear when heat comes," I expected Christianity to be the life of peace and joy she exuded.

As an adult looking back on my grandmother's short life, I can see her struggles. I understand the pain that accompanied those crippled fingers and the bills associated with long hospital stays. Now I realize working twenty hours each week at minimum wage just barely paid the bills. On the other hand, I am also keenly aware that my grandmother lived the Jeremiah 17 life.

Grandma trusted God and lived by the power of the Holy Spirit. No matter what life threw her way, she stood firm on Christ. I'm guessing she vented to her close friends, but she didn't allow trouble to bring her down. She understood the heat of life is a refiner's fire. It doesn't damage; it makes us better.

So as we face the day to day heat of the fire, whether it's the fire from the world or the one Christ sends to refine us, trust Him. Trust allows us to stand, to be joyful in affliction and feel blessed during times of trial. Confidence in our maker enables us to see the refiner's fire so we can take the heat.

A New, Better, More Beautiful You

Therefore, if anyone is in Christ,
the new creation has come:
The old has gone, the new is here!
2 Corinthians 5:17 (NIV)

He who was seated on the throne said,
"I am making everything new!"
Revelation 21:5 (NIV)

Jesus says He makes us new, but I wonder if I'm in the market for a remodel or a rebuild. Let's face it, when we consider giving our home a new look, it's easier to slap on a coat of paint and replace the carpet than tear the walls down and start over. From a building standpoint it doesn't make sense to rebuild when the structure appears to be just fine.

However, when it comes to the human condition, Jesus says He wants a rebuild. Take it all down and put up something new. What a scary thought!

Becoming new sounds exciting, yet we all have parts we'd like to hold on to. We try to convince Jesus we don't need a whole new building; adding a wing will be enough. Our electrical system is fine, let's just change out the cabinets and flooring. But Jesus is a contractor who does all or nothing.

That's not to say He won't ever use the old to form the new. Just like churches will sometimes take stained glass windows from century old buildings when they put up something more modern, Jesus might choose to save the most beautiful parts when His Spirit remolds us. Our dilemma arises when we discover we don't get a say in which parts He remakes and which ones He discards.

Each day, week, month, year, and season offer times to start over. We're sure we're going to do it better this time! But how often do we forget to ask the Master Carpenter what His blueprints look like in this time of renewal?

Jesus isn't looking for the improved you. He doesn't need the recently remodeled, updated version. Our Savior is waiting for the willing you, the broken, but eager to be rebuilt, humbled you. And as He begins making everything new, you'll start to know the peace that comes from not doing it alone. Let's give up the do-it-yourself resolutions so Christ can recreate us and make us into exactly what He originally created us to be.

Support for Missionaries

19 Therefore go and make disciples of all nations,
baptizing them in the name
of the Father and of the Son and of the Holy Spirit,
20 and teaching them to obey
everything I have commanded you.
And surely I am with you always,
to the very end of the age."
Matthew 28:19-20 (NIV)

When my sister went on her first mission trip, I prayed for her every day. As I prayed, I journaled so I could give her a memory of her first mission trip. I admire her so much because I've never been on a mission trip. Or at least that's what I thought.

During my prayer time Jesus reminded me of something He told me years ago. You see, it's not that I've never considered going into some remote area of the world to take the message of Jesus Christ. I pray about it often. But so far, Christ hasn't asked me to use a passport to share the gospel.

My excitement for my sister to become a short-term missionary, reminded me of my call to be a long-term missionary. Right here – where I am. Jesus instructed His followers to "Go and make disciples of all nations . . ." And if we check out Acts, we'll see He told them to be witnesses in Jerusalem, as well as Judea, Samaria, and the ends of the earth. Someone had to be the missionary in Jerusalem. Some had to stay home and share the gospel.

I am thankful for those who travel overseas to share the love of Jesus

Christ. I personally sponsor two children through World Vision, one in Bolivia and one in Guatemala, so they can know Jesus. However, Christ reminded me He values those who stay in Jerusalem just as much as those who go to the ends of the earth.

Every follower of Jesus Christ is called to be a missionary of sorts. Some will be led to go to Thailand and India, Honduras, and Mozambique. But others will have an even tougher mission field at McDonald's and Wendy's. There's the mission field at the office and the one at the mall. Some care for the prostitutes near their church, and others feed the hungry close to home. Much like foreign missionaries, we won't need to know so much Bible we quote Jesus like a theologian. Instead we'll focus on being the hands and feet of Christ so others wonder how anyone can show so much love.

My sister's jaunt out of the country spurred me to focus more on my mission field. I lead Bible Study and teach Sunday School every week. My devotions and curriculum go all over the world. Cards of encouragement show Christ's love to the young people in our congregation, and I try to be a living witness to the beauty of Christ every place I go. I'll always keep my ears and heart open to the possibility that Christ may send me to Mexico or Zimbabwe, but meanwhile, I'll strive to be all Christ has created me to be right here in my Jerusalem making as many disciples as possible in this little part of all the nations.

When God is in Control

Be Still and Know that I am God
Psalm 46:10 (NIV)

My 1990 journal records a Friday night I was supposed to hear
Carmen in concert. The six members of my band and our families arranged to
travel together on our old converted school bus. But plans change.

The evening before I'd spent most of the night on the floor of the
bathroom with a bucket. I prayed and begged my Heavenly Father to take the
illness away. My notebook says,

> *"I believe in my heart had He chosen to do so,*
> *He could have, and I wasn't sure why He chose not to,*
> *but I finally just gave it to Him to do with as He pleased.*
> *(And He still pleased NOT to take it away.)"*

That Thursday started horribly. I'm not a morning person, but I
woke early so I could stop at my mom's for a shower. We'd been without
water for at least 36 hours. My job consumed me, and my family dictated all
my free time. Teary eyes and prayers for help filled the half-hour drive to
work. My journal recalls,

> *"My music has gotten lost in the shuffle. Where will it end?*
> *I manage to make time for hurried prayers,*
> *and I wearily read my Bible, but I find myself crying out*
> *for God's help to slow things down*
> *and give me some control of my life.*

The only thing keeping me sane at this point
are the words of praise He's taught me
to lift up to Him in times of trial."

I believe God's tardiness in answering what I called my "bucket prayer" those decades ago allowed him to answer my commuting cries. If healing had come early Thursday evening, I'd have gone to work Friday morning. Within minutes of getting home, the family would have loaded on the bus to get to the concert on time. I would have been exhausted. And according to my little journal, several of my own concerts on Saturday and Sunday as well as a nine-year old's birthday on Monday required my attention.

I wanted to slow down, but it seemed impossible. I realize God doesn't cause illness; however, He used this malady to give my thirty-something self a valuable message. Listen to it from her perspective:

"In the recovery time the illness forced me to take,
I heard God's voice.
I was awake much of last night
and in bed until two this afternoon.
During this time my Savior spoke to me,
and I realized this illness was really His gift.
I couldn't seem to slow down, so He slowed me down.
Hopefully I learned a lesson today,
one I won't quickly forget,
and one that God won't need to teach me again.
What exactly is that lesson? Let God be in control.
When life gets too hectic and seems out of control,
it probably is, so give it back to Him."

The Burden of the Old Covenant

15 And the Levites carried the ark of God
with the poles on their shoulders,
as Moses had commanded in accordance
with the word of the LORD.
1 Chronicles 15:15 (NIV)

When I read this verse, I picture four men carrying a long narrow wooden container covered with gold. According to Elihu Schatz[ii], this holy box with two angels on the lid weighed more than 180 pounds. And scripture tells us the Levites carried the it all over the desert for nearly 40 years. That's a lot of weight to lug around.

The Ark was the symbol of God's covenant with His chosen people. It held Aaron's rod and the tablets with the commandments. The Israelites believed God's presence rested on the Ark, and they revered it. But just like the covenant it represented, the 180-pound box burdened those priests in charge of protecting and transporting it to the next location.

The Old Covenant had its foundation in the rules. Right standing with the Creator came through obedience. And although God made it clear, on more than one occasion, He concerned Himself more with the condition of the heart than the worth of the sacrifice, few Israelites seemed to be able to live up to either.

For thousands of years, God's chosen tried to find abundance in the cumbersome law. They searched for what only Jesus could give. His death on the cross and His resurrection unleashed the Holy Spirit. Christ removed the burden of the Old Covenant and lifted the weight of the Ark.

When we consider the burden of the Ark of the Covenant, the freedom of Christ's New Covenant becomes even more amazing. Romans 8:21 says we were "liberated from sin's bondage and brought into the freedom and glory of God." 2 Corinthians 3:17 tells us "where the Spirit of the Lord is there is freedom." In Galatians Paul reminds us we are children of the free woman instead of the slave. And John tells us the "truth will set us free" and if the "Son sets us free; we are free indeed."

Because of these great promises, when I hear folks list the requirements of Christianity, I feel distraught. Some think they have to go to church. Others have to be nice. The poles of the Ark rest on their shoulders. They live under the weight of the rules instead of the freedom of the relationship.

Unfortunately, almost everyone picks up the Ark from time to time. When we focus on what others expect rather God's plan, we pick up the Ark. Everything we're "supposed" to do keeps us from the openness and beauty of living in the freedom of Christ. These self-imposed obligations become our Ark, a weight hanging around a Christian's neck.

God created us for relationship, not rules. It's time to drop the Ark of the Old Covenant and pick up the Promise of the New Covenant. Jesus said His yoke is easy and His burden is light. Let's not allow the weight of the shoulds keep us from the joy of living in the love of Christ.

What Do Your Prayers Smell Like?

$\sim\!\!\!\sim\!\!\!\sim\!\!\!\sim\!\!\!\sim\!\!\!\sim\!\!\!\sim\!\!\!\sim$

> [7] "Aaron must burn fragrant incense on the altar
> every morning when he tends the lamps.
> [8] He must burn incense again
> when he lights the lamps at twilight
> so incense will burn regularly before the LORD
> for the generations to come.
> Exodus 30:7-8 (NIV)

> [8] And when he had taken it,
> the four living creatures
> and the twenty-four elders fell down before the Lamb.
> Each one had a harp,
> and they were holding golden bowls full of incense,
> which are the prayers of God's people.
> Revelation 5:8 (NIV)

God instructed the priests to bring new incense into the temple every morning and evening. I picture a bowl full of special resin burning for hours. Filled twice a day, the sweet-smelling fragrance continuously wafted to the heavens.

Exodus and Leviticus recorded so many rituals like this. From a twenty-first century perspective, they seem pointless. After all, if they were so important, why don't God followers still practice them today?

But like many Old Testament acts of worship, the New Testament reveals God's heart in the matter. The incense offered by the priests foreshadows the bowls held by the twenty-four elders in Revelation 5.

John reminds us our prayers are a sweet-smelling fragrance to the Almighty. Is it a coincidence most of us learn young to offer morning and bedtime prayers?

Unfortunately, many folks pray as if they're burning a small incense stick, a few minutes when they wake and a one or two more before bed. They might throw in a line or two before they eat, but does this kind of prayer life mimic the incense of the temple?

In 1 Thessalonians 5:17 Paul reminds us to pray continuously. Like the priestly offering, God wants to hear from us throughout the day. Words of praise when we open our eyes as well as intercession for loved ones in the middle of the night smell beautiful to our Heavenly Father. The fragrance of our honest cries for help seem as sweet to our Creator as grateful thanks for His handiwork.

At least twice each day our prayers should be a reminder of the incense Aaron's descendants brought into the Holy place. I hope to never forget John's imagery of the prayers of the saints. May our Savior find your prayers to be just as sweet and long lasting.

God is Not Slow

The Lord is not slow in keeping his promise,
as some understand slowness.
He is patient with you, not wanting anyone to perish,
but everyone to come to repentance.
2 Peter 3:9 (NIV)

Some days my internet just barely works. Because I work from my living room out in the country, I use a hotspot rather than traditional broadband. Generally it gets the job done (although I wouldn't mind having enough bandwidth to get Netflix)[iii], but when it doesn't work, I feel frustrated. I click refresh over and over to no avail. Even restarting my computer and hotspot won't help. As my frustration rises, my heavenly Father reminds me of all the times He waits.

Peter tells us, "God isn't slow as some of you might think, he's just patient." Our instant gratification culture spoils us. We want things to happen now, but much of what we think should occur immediately has no Kingdom value. God, on the other hand, only concerns Himself with those things that impact His realm, and His time reference is sometime before Christ returns. As a Christian, God's priorities should be my priority. So, if God's primary focus is that none should perish, you can guess what mine should be.

So as I sit there, using my printed Bible instead of online scripture, a convenience I've come to truly enjoy, I think about the times I become impatient. Slow cashiers, my empty glass at a restaurant, traffic lights, standing in lines, so many scenarios of irritation brought on by a few seconds of tardiness.

But what if God hadn't waited on me. What if He given me only one chance to come to Him? How would my life be different if He hadn't been patient when I was slow to grow or understand His Word? On more than one occasion an "aha" moment led to the realization God had been speaking the lesson to me for weeks or months.

All my contemplation begs the questions, "Do I show others the same patience my Heavenly Father gave me?" Am I more concerned about the things of the Kingdom of God than I am the speed of my internet connection?

Christ isn't slow in keeping His promises. He waited on me to follow Him, to be His friend. Jesus has shown me an abundance of love, kindness, and patience. I pray I can pass His goodness on to others so they can know the beautiful patience of the One who loves us more than we can imagine.

Search Me . . . Try Me . . . Maybe?

²³ Search me, O God, and know my heart:
try me, and know my thoughts:
²⁴ And see if there be any wicked way in me,
and lead me in the way everlasting.
Psalm 139:23-24 (KJV)

More than a few songs feature this short prayer from King David. Some can even quote them with chapter and verse, and many recognize they're from the Psalms. Despite their familiarity, I believe we read these verses too passively.

I like to pray the Psalms, paraphrasing to make them personal. This one needs little transcribing, "Search my heart, Lord; test me, Father. You know my thoughts. Look deep inside and see if there is any wickedness in me. Lead me so I can have eternal life."

But I wonder, "Do we really want our Creator to test us?"

I've read about God's tests, and I'm afraid I'd fail! Job lost everything . . . Peter denied Christ . . . Paul found himself in prison. None seem like much fun. It brings to mind the old saying, "Be careful what you pray for."

Verse twenty-four sums it up, "see if there be any wicked way in me." Most of us who've been good rule followers don't really relate to the "wicked" part of that verse. Our parents taught us about wickedness, and we've steered clear of it longer than we can remember.

Isaiah, however, sheds a different light on our goodness. He said our righteousness looks like dirty rags to God. (Isaiah 64:6) If that's the case, I need to take a new look at wickedness. Other scripture versions translate it as offensive and hurtful. The Hebrew lexicon defines it as something that causes pain.

Most of us avoid offensive or hurtful behavior. We don't want to cause anyone pain. So again, it becomes easy to pray these words and move on.

But as we consider all Christ has done for us, we might do well to ask if we've caused our Heavenly Father any pain. Have I offended the One who gave me life? Compared to other humans, I'm definitely not wicked, but compared to the perfection of Christ . . .

Yeah . . . me too . . .

I've discovered I cannot appreciate the sacrifice Christ made on my behalf until I realize I wasn't worth dying for. God didn't show me this to make me feel shame or belittle myself. But without recognizing all that separates me from Christ, I'm not able to turn from it. My Savior knows as I begin to see the "wicked way in me," the power of Jesus' blood cleanses and sets me free! Only through the discovery of what's wicked can we appreciate the righteousness Jesus gives and follow Him down the path of everlasting life.

Making Deals with God

When Jephthah returned home . . .
his daughter came out to meet him dancing . . .
When he saw her, he tore his clothes and cried . . .
"because I have made
a vow to the Lord that I cannot break."
Judges 11:34-35

If you're not familiar with this story, check out Judges 11

For many years I struggled with Jephthah's story. He made a deal with God. If he won the battle, he promised to sacrifice the first thing that greeted him when he returned home. However, when his daughter runs out the door, Jephthah tears his clothes in distress.

I didn't understand. How could the God I know, serve, and love with all my heart, ask a man to sacrifice his daughter as payment for helping him defeat his enemies? Why would God accept such a deal? Each time I read Judges, I preferred to ignore chapter 11. I didn't want to deal with those difficult verses.

If you've never read (or paid attention to) the story of Jephthah the judge, I encourage you to read this short chapter. You may feel bad for the young girl who simply wanted to greet her successful warrior father. Jephthah's story raises so many questions, including, "Why would you make such a promise when you know it will be your daughter or wife who comes out to greet you?"

And that is the question that finally helped me with my struggle. Why do we make deals with God? The Almighty didn't ask Jephthah to give up his only daughter in exchange for the win. God pre-arranged Israel's victory. To change His plan, even to avoid the death of Jephthah's daughter, would not have played into God's bigger picture.

With each page turn in Judges, we see Israel spinning more and more out of control. Every judge walked a bit further from God, and Jephthah arrives on the scene near the end of the succession.

This judge's vow reminded me of all the noble promises people make to God every day. "If You will _____, I will . . ." But our Creator doesn't barter. He has only one deal, and He repeats it in a variety of ways throughout scripture. "If you love me, you will keep my commandments." (John 14:15) "If you will follow me with all your heart as David did, I will bless you." (1 Kings 3:14) "If my people . . . will . . . pray . . . I will hear from heaven." (2 Chronicles 7:14) "If you believe in my Son, you'll have eternal life." (John 3:16)

God doesn't want hollow sacrifices and rash promises. He wants love and obedience. Since the Garden of Eden, our Maker only asks for authentic relationship. He doesn't need our deals. If we simply accept the terms He's already set, that will be enough.

I admire Jephthah's willingness to keep his word even when his heart was breaking. Those who make promises to the Almighty should be prepared to back them up. I prefer, however, to just walk in His will, to simply be His friend and trust He will always do what's best for me, deal or no deal.

The Cure for Tired

Come to me ... and I will give you rest.
Matthew 11:28 (NIV)

As I thumb through my old journals, the word tired keeps popping out. I wish my younger self had read the devotional "My Utmost for His Highest," but perhaps the 30-something me lacked the maturity to grasp the wisdom of Oswald Chambers.

In one of his sermons, Chambers reminds us Jesus wants to "re-establish our rest." He challenges me to abandon self and run to my Savior to find a peace that escapes most Christians. I wonder if "Lynne of the journal" would have understood finding complete rest in Christ.

In 1998, speculation filled my journal pages. I didn't doubt Christ; I doubted myself. At least once a week I wrote, "I want to obey God, but I wonder if I am." I know Jesus said, "Seek and you will find." Yet, in all my seeking, I don't remember a lot of finding!

My heart reveals itself in those old journals. I longed to know the will of God, but self-examination was the overarching theme. Oswald Chambers described it as self-awareness that awakens self-pity, and in my case, leads to feeling tired. I spent so much time trying to fix myself I overlooked the fact Christ was already taking care of the job.

Chambers says, "If we try to overcome our self-awareness through any of our own commonsense methods, we will only serve to strengthen our self-awareness tremendously."[iv] I excel in commonsense methods! Each journal entry featured a deep desire to serve my Heavenly Father followed by a commonsense search for my next step. I sought a fix instead of seeking

Him, and I missed out on His rest.

My twenty-year old journal confirms Mr. Chambers' wisdom. Today my children are grown. Instead of keeping up with three growing girls, I amble behind an aging senior citizen. Children were easier, yet I'm much less weary because I've discovered the rest that comes from seeking Christ.

When I work to make myself Christ-like, I get tired. But when I simply come to Christ, get to know Him more and live in His love, I find rest.

Mean What You Say and Say What You Mean

...do I make my plans in a worldly manner
so that in the same breath
I say both "Yes, yes" and "No, no"?
[18] But as surely as God is faithful,
our message to you is not "Yes" and "No."
2 Corinthians 1:12-24 (NLT)

"Mean what you say or say what you mean." My dad repeated that phrase often. I tease my mom for asking things like, "Do you have to work tomorrow?" when what she really wants to know is "Are you free for lunch?" because one doesn't necessarily preclude the other.

So many throw around the word "starving." I challenge our youth group when they say it. Thanks to mission projects we understand better what starving truly means, so we've been able to curtail its use.

Everyone says things they don't mean, and most of us exaggerate to the point we muddle the truth. You can count on a few RSVP's being no shows, and some folks only get asked to volunteer for jobs that can be easily covered. Sadly, when we find someone whose word we trust implicitly, it's a rare jewel.

Tragically, the church is not exempt. Those who make hasty decisions or volunteer out of a desire to please, often leave us hanging. Whether it's a promise to lead children, gather supplies or simply be in attendance, when we give our word, someone depends on us.

Occasionally we'll find ourselves in a predicament like Paul. Unforeseen circumstances force us to change plans. However, when this happens on a regular basis, our promises become hollow and our witness weakens. In more than one place, Scripture tells us to consider our words, always let our "yes" be "yes." It's important we "mean what we say."

Our careless use of phrases like "you're killing me" and "starving" are harmless. Most folks understand. However, these idioms make great reminders. As followers of Christ, people should be able to rely on our word. When we commit to doing something, our friends should consider it done. "Trustworthy and true to his word" should be a slogan that describes us. Like Paul, our plans may change, but it should be the exception, not the rule.

When someone asks you to do a task, in or outside the church, don't answer hastily. May each word be spoken only after prayerful consideration. As surely as God is faithful, let your "yes" mean "yes" in Jesus Christ.

More Than I can Ask or Imagine

[20] *Now to him who is able to do*
immeasurably more than all we ask or imagine,
according to his power that is at work within us,
[21] *to him be glory in the church*
and in Christ Jesus throughout all generations,
for ever and ever! Amen.
Ephesians 3:20-21 (NIV)

I love this benediction from Paul. The God who loves me with an
unending love has the power to do more than I can ask or even imagine. His
abilities go beyond what I can measure. We see proof in the story of
Shadrach, Meshach, and Abednego in the fiery furnace.

Daniel 3 paints a picture of three wise men standing before the king.
Respected leaders one day, tied up and threatened for their faith the next.
And I wonder . . . when the trio told King Nebuchadnezzar Yahweh had their
back, were they trying to guess how God might rescue them from the fire?
Or is that just my M.O.?

Whenever I find myself in a tough spot, I start asking my Father to
rescue me. Then I begin to imagine the different ways He could give me
assistance. Sometimes, when I forget this verse from Ephesians, I even
include the scenarios in my prayer, as if God needed my ideas to get me out of
a bind that I probably put myself in.

Daniel's friends stayed calm when they faced the fiery furnace after
refusing to bow to the king's statue. But I'm guessing their human nature had
some creative approaches to their imminent rescue. Maybe they imagined

someone reminding Nebuchadnezzar of the dream God had given him. Or perhaps they thought the Creator would instigate a nice diversion. But did it ever cross their minds, they would walk around in a fire so hot it killed the guys who threw them in? In their wildest dreams could they have possibly envisioned the One who looked like the "Son of a God" strolling in the heat with them? I think God described their clothing in such detail to help us understand the magnitude of the rescue. Robes, trousers, turbans and more, yet not one little singe. How could anyone predict this kind of amazing spectacle?

  Shadrach, Meshach, and Abednego's ordeal reminds me to keep my prayers simple and let God come up with the ideas. Occasionally our Heavenly Father tells us ahead of time what He plans to do, like Elijah on the mountain with the prophets of Baal[2]. During those times, our prayers should be big and specific. But I have discovered that most often I need to speak more like Shadrach, Meshach, and Abednego. Even though I have no idea how God will come through, I can be confident He will. I only know whatever He does it will be immeasurably more than I can ask or imagine.

---

[2] 1 Kings 18

Become Part of the Band

Now if the foot should say,
"Because I am not a hand, I do not belong to the body,"
it would not for that reason stop being part of the body.
And if the ear should say,
"Because I am not an eye, I do not belong to the body,"
it would not for that reason stop being part of the body.
But in fact God has placed the parts in the body,
every one of them, just as he wanted them to be.
1 Corinthians 12:15-16 & 18 (NIV)

My oldest grandchildren perform with the best high school band I've ever heard. We've lived in five different school districts, so I've got a few to compare it to. They memorize each piece and play with precision. Recently at an event with less than 50 people in attendance, they played a full thirty minutes as if performing to a packed house, and they looked like they were having fun!

Their performance reminded me of these verses from 1 Corinthians. Each of those teens played their part with gusto. The harmonies blended so well an untrained ear may not have noticed all the unique parts. Every person played their best, but no one tried to outdo the others.

A great high school band exemplifies Paul's message. Like the instruments in an orchestra, every player in the Kingdom is invaluable. Often we live like only the first chair deserves recognition; however, even a virtuoso's solo performance becomes dull after the first couple numbers. To keep the crowd entertained, she needs the harmonies and rhythms of other musicians, professionals who've perfected their craft.

We live in a world where mediocrity reigns. The "It's Good Enough" mentality infiltrates schools and workplaces. Fortunately, it gives the church a great opportunity to live differently.

Might we perform better if we remember Christ needs our part? What would we volunteer for if we believed we were created to contribute? Will our actions demonstrate to the next generation no player is too small and every tingle of the triangle vital to the beauty of the Composer's masterpiece?

We have a choice to make.

Will we sit back and let the soloists do all the work? It's going to get boring soon. Perhaps this is the reason church attendance is falling off. Without each person playing their part with passion, the music gets stale, no one wants to listen.

Instead let's embrace the truth. We have been created with gifts and talents, each a beautiful motif the body of Christ needs to complete our magnificent sonata. The orchestra needs me. And they need you. Every shake of the egg, each pluck of the bass, whatever part you've been chosen to play, the concert won't be the same without you!

Making it Personal

^{24} *He got up and rebuked the wind and the raging waters;*
the storm subsided, and all was calm.
^{25} *"Where is your faith?" he asked his disciples.*
In fear and amazement they asked one another,
"Who is this?
He commands even the winds and the water,
and they obey him."
Luke 8:24-25 (NIV)

This passage causes me to scratch my head. I know it's early in Jesus' ministry, but seriously! The apostles had seen the centurion's servant healed and the widow's son raised from the dead. Four of them experienced a catch of fish big enough to make them leave the family business, and a few saw Jesus heal a leper. Surely, they'd all heard about the paralyzed man walking. Still it takes a life-threatening storm to help them understand their new friend is more than just a Godly carpenter.

Not much has changed in 2000 years. What must Christ do for humans today to help them really understand the "who" of Jesus? After walking with Christ and experiencing His blessings, do we understand the weight of His personality? Will seeing our Messiah work in mystifying ways help us view His abilities with wonderment or appreciate His graciousness with us?

Jesus' ability amazed the twelve. They feared for their lives in that small boat; then Jesus' power touched them, marking the beginning of their transformation. As they began to allow Jesus' blessings to become truly personal, their amazement turned from "Who is this?" to "Who am I that He would grant me this?" Like the disciples, we must grow to the point his abilities no longer surprise us because we know who Jesus is. Instead we stand in awe He counts us worthy.

As I toss that thought around, my grandmother comes to mind. She had a humble, yet extraordinarily large faith. I believe she took every blessing personally. I can't know whether she learned the skill early in life or discovered it after she witnessed the birth of all four grandchildren, despite doctors' warning she'd succumb to Lupus before we got here. The Christ who calmed winds and wave granted her extra years on earth, and by the time the disease took her, just before my seventeenth birthday, the love of Jesus Christ continually leaked out of her.

I try to look at every blessing my Savior bestows with reverence and gratefulness. Yes, he is able to do more than I can ask or imagine. But should it surprise me when he does? I pray my surprise always changes to amazement because He often counts me worthy to be a part of such things.

What's Next?

⁶ Then they gathered around him and asked him,
"Lord, are you at this time going to restore the kingdom to Israel?"

⁷ He said to them: "It is not for you to know the times
or dates the Father has set by his own authority.
⁸ But you will receive power
when the Holy Spirit comes on you;
and you will be my witnesses in Jerusalem,
and in all Judea and Samaria,
and to the ends of the earth."
Acts 1:6-8 (NIV)

What's next? Everyone wants to know. Opinions regarding what God should or will do abound. Most find their inspiration from cut and paste scripture rather than the wisdom of the entire book. I think the narrow question the crowd asked Jesus sprang from that same kind of cherry picking.

With limited access to the book itself, the Jewish community relied on priests to pass on scriptural knowledge. Either these leaders limited their teaching to the hope of a conquering Messiah, or the people clung to those promises and missed the light to the Gentiles parts. The majority wanted Jesus to lead a military coup.

Today the book of Revelation brings the most inquiries. When will it take place? Will Jesus take us before the tribulation? And everyone wants to know about the future. Where will God take me in ten years? Does Christ want me to be a missionary?

Our Creator answered all those questions in Acts. It's not for us to know the times, dates or even the details. We're called to rest in the power of the Holy Spirit, to go out in that Spirit and be witnesses to all that Jesus has done in our lives. Unfortunately, we don't like those answers anymore than the Jews enjoyed hearing God was making a way for the foreigners.

We want details, but it's only occasionally our Heavenly Father offers the particulars. He revealed to Ananias Saul's future proclaiming Christ among the Gentiles. (Acts 9) And after Saul became Paul, God showed him he needed to go to Macedonia. (Acts 16)

More often, though, there's no advance warning. Peter didn't know he was supposed to go talk to the centurion until the servant arrived at his doorstep. (Acts 10) Philip wasn't given a heads up that he would meet an Ethiopian and then be air-lifted to Azotus. (Acts 8) Still, all four listened closely to hear the Holy Spirit, and they let the power of Christ work in them. Ananias, Paul, Peter, and Philip each waited anxiously to be a witness to our Savior's grace.

These verses force me to evaluate my own questions. Do I miss what Christ is doing in my life today because I'm busy trying to figure out what's next? Am I looking for what the future holds more often than I seek the power of the Holy Spirit? It's tempting to build preconceived notions of what we think God should do. Instead our focus should be on what He puts before us. Like Peter and Philip, I want to be aware of how I can show Jesus to the man at the door or the guy reading a book by the lake. Let me always walk in the power of the Spirit so I can be His witness in my hometown and my nation. And maybe, if He takes me . . . to the ends of the earth.

I am Weak, but He is Strong

³ For what the law was powerless to do
because it was weakened by the flesh,
God did by sending his own Son
in the likeness of sinful flesh to be a sin offering.
Romans 8:3 (NIV)

I own a book of devotions excerpted from John Wesley's sermons. In one sermon Mr. Wesley points out the folly in trying to be saved by following the law. No matter how closely we adhere to them, the principles laid out in scripture will not make a place for us in the Kingdom of Heaven. For many that truth is hard to swallow.

But Mr. Wesley's words remind me of another truth. Like the law, I cannot save anyone. Like the law, I am powerless. Though they follow me or mimic my life, they'll still miss life abundant and a home with my Heavenly Father.

Often I invest time and energy into discipling a person. After building a relationship, studying scripture with them, praying with and for them, I find myself disappointed when they don't accept Christ or grow as quickly as I think they should. Then I remember, I am not a savior.

Paul said the law helped him see his sin, but it couldn't provide deliverance. Much like preachers and teachers; we can reveal sin and bestow knowledge of sin, but only the Trinity frees us from sin. When we cling to a human, expecting them to get us in good with the Father, we might as well hold on to the law for salvation.

The law is powerless, and I am too. Keeping that in mind as I share the gospel gives me freedom. Like the law, I am weak, but that's OK, because as the familiar child's song says, "He is strong."

You Can Please Some of the People Some of the Time

Nevertheless, many did believe in Him
even among the rulers,
but because of the Pharisees
they did not confess Him,
so they would not be banned
from the synagogue.
For they loved praise from men
more than praise from God.
John 12:42-43 (HCSB)

I am a people pleaser. I avoid conflict like the plague and worry way too much what others think, especially about me personally. As a child, and even into my teens, I earned the label "goodie-two shoes." In the recovery circle, they call it co-dependent.

There, I've said it! It's out there. Now I should be able to get on with my life and live in complete obedience to Jesus Christ. But I've confessed before, and even though I see progress, the opinion of others still carries too much weight.

When someone I care about questions my motives or actions, it troubles me. And I've sat in a pew before many performances worrying what the crowd will think of my songs or my message. No matter how much I pray about it, regardless of the assurance my Heavenly Father loves me, I continue to contemplate the variety of ways to garner approval from the humans in my

Devotions Inspired by Life | 73

life.

I obviously can't completely dismiss others' feelings or opinions; that would be arrogant. However, I wish I could learn to focus fully on the Holy Spirit's constant whisper in my ear, "Why does it matter what they think?"

After twenty years I win the struggle more often than I lose. I'm so grateful for my Savior's soft voice. Listening to His stirring and appreciating the Father's opinion brings peace when the crowd doesn't approve. The lives of Jesus, Peter, Paul, and the rest remind me this life is not a popularity contest. While the Psalms and the Cross assure me, I'm quite popular with the only One whose opinion really matters!

Do You have a Spring or a Cistern?

My people have committed two sins:
They have forsaken me, the spring of living water,
and have dug their own cisterns,
broken cisterns that cannot hold water.
Jeremiah 2:13 (NIV)

I wonder if today's generation, with water pumped from a filtration system, truly appreciates these words of Jeremiah. I grew up on a farm with a spring. No matter how dry the season, we never ran out of water, and it always ran cold. Several springs in our area have been harnessed. Pipes coming out of the hill invite the world to fill jugs from these cool clear sources.

On the other hand, my aunt had a cistern. During dry seasons we used her water sparingly because if it ran dry an expensive water tanker would have to fill it. A jug in the refrigerator provided cool refreshment because her tap felt more lukewarm.

Spring water rushes through rocks deep in the earth making it pure and cool. It moves constantly. Cistern water sits there. It may stir a bit when rain runs in, but for the most part it remains still and warm.

In Jeremiah's day men dug huge holes for cisterns, lining them with clay to keep the water from soaking into the soil. Today a metal tank fills the cavern. Either way cisterns take a lot of work. Conversely springs occur naturally and require little effort to harness. Even in our world of technology and filters, bottled spring water remains a favorite.

So, when God says we forsake Him, the Spring of Living Water, by digging our own cisterns, he's describing something that in my childhood would have been considered foolish. No one who had a good spring on their property would dig a cistern.

Nowadays springs and cisterns are obsolete. Most folks get a monthly bill in the mail for the privilege of drinking water supplied by some municipality. When God addresses our spiritual supply, perhaps he'd ask if it comes from the city or the Spring.

John tells us Jesus offers a spring of Living Water.[3] But just like the people in Jeremiah's time, many attempt to find peace and refreshment in the world's water supply. Others try digging their own cisterns, one shovelful at a time. These folks work hard and end up settling for stagnant, warm water, missing out on the pure, cool Springs available at no cost to everyone who truly believes.

---

[3] John 4:14

Don't Blame the Groundhog

Leviticus 16

I live in Ohio not far from the Pennsylvania state line, just 125 miles from the small town of Punxsutawney. With less than 6,000 residents, this town would've never made the news without their famous groundhog, Phil.

Every February 2 men dressed in top hats and tails wake the poor rodent and drag him out of his hole. If the little guy sees his shadow and retreats into his den, which he usually does, legend says we'll have six more weeks of winter. And then the bashing begins.

I feel sorry for the furry fellow! Do people think he controls the weather? I'm puzzled why we started blaming a groundhog for the calendar, as if it's his fault spring doesn't begin till March 21. Maybe someone thought it was sacrilegious to blame God, so they came up with another victim. And now with social media, the groundhog takes even more heat. It's just not fair.

But poor Phil is your typical scapegoat.

Many don't understand the truth of the scapegoat. Most don't even know the term originated in the Bible. We use it to describe a person who took the fall for someone else. Kind of like Pennsylvania's favorite rodent taking responsibility for a winter that lasts until spring.

Leviticus 16 explains the concept:

⁵ [The priest] is to take two male goats for a sin offering and a ram for a burnt offering...

⁹ Aaron shall bring the goat whose lot falls to the LORD and sacrifice it for a sin offering.

¹⁰ But the goat chosen by lot as the scapegoat shall be presented alive before the LORD to be used for making atonement by sending it into the wilderness as a scapegoat...

²⁰ *"When Aaron has finished making atonement for the Most Holy Place, the tent of meeting and the altar...*²¹ *He is to lay both hands on the head of the live goat and confess over it all the wickedness and rebellion of the Israelites—all their sins—and put them on the goat's head...* ²² *The goat will carry on itself all their sins to a remote place;*

Humans don't like to admit we're wrong, so we appreciate the scapegoat. It's easy to find someone or something else to blame. But down through the ages, we've lost the true beauty of the scapegoat. The priest confessed all of Israel's sins and rebellion over the goat so they could be carried to a remote place. Never meant to hide or excuse sin, God meant for the scapegoat to be a physical reminder that He wants to remove all sin. The scapegoat foreshadowed Jesus.

Making excuses for bad behavior or trying to cover it up can't take away sin any more than Phil can grant an early spring. When we throw around blame and deny our part, we can't escape it or ever be free. Fortunately for us Jesus came to be our scapegoat.

However, when we confess the things that separate us from our Heavenly Father, Jesus takes our sin upon Him and carries it into the wilderness. We are free from it forever. Christ, the scapegoat, fulfills the promise of Psalm 103.

> *"His love for His followers reaches as high as the heavens,*
> *and He has taken away our sin as far as the east is from the west."*

Looking for God

You, God, are my God, earnestly I seek you;
I thirst for you, my whole being longs for you,
in a dry and parched land where there is no water
Psalm 63:1 (NIV)

But if from there you seek the Lord your God,
you will find him if you seek him
with all your heart and with all your soul
Deuteronomy 4:29 (NIV)

Every child loves to play Hide and Seek. Teeny ones find Peek-a-Boo hilarious. When did we stop enjoying the hunt? I'm guessing the thrill starts to wane the first time a shoe comes up missing. And it's never fun looking for a hairbrush when you're getting ready for school. Lost keys make us late, and when our cell phone goes into hiding, we pray someone calls. The seeking and finding that brought laughs and fun at age five becomes frustrating by the time we're twenty-five.

Seeking steals precious time, and it seems like things wait to go missing when it's time to walk out the door. Our busy schedules don't include time to investigate the whereabouts of necessities that should be at our fingertips. Yet God asks us to seek Him.

Explore, pursue, follow, and inquire are synonyms of seek. The Psalmist used the words thirst and long for to describe his desperate need for the Almighty. But how often do we chase after Jesus with the same passion we use to track down lost keys? Do we read scripture with the same diligence as complicated assembly instructions? When the precious items of life are lost, we go into stealth mode until they're found. But what if we employed the same effort in seeking God?

The irony of the situation is God doesn't hide; He stands in plain view. Your Heavenly Father wants to be found. We don't see Him because we're too busy looking for everything else.

At least ten verses in the Bible tell us to seek God. The most famous is Matthew 6:33:

> *Seek first the Kingdom of God and His righteousness,*
> *and all you need will be given to you.*

When we earnestly seek God with all the energy we normally use to find our keys, everything else falls into place. In fact, on more than one occasion after I've spent time with Jesus, He showed me the hiding place of a lost something I needed for the day. Keys, clothing, hubcaps. Christ has helped me find them all.

Today let's be like the Psalmist. Let's use every bit of our being to seek the Living Water so we can find refreshment in this dry, parched land.

It's Like Yeast and Seeds

[decorative divider]

¹⁸ Then Jesus asked, "What is the kingdom of God like?
What shall I compare it to?
¹⁹ It is like a mustard seed,
which a man took and planted in his garden.
It grew and became a tree,
and the birds perched in its branches."

²⁰ Again he asked,
"What shall I compare the kingdom of God to?
²¹ It is like yeast that a woman took
and mixed into about sixty pounds of flour
until it worked all through the dough."
Luke 13:18-21 (NIV)

You should see the notebook I use when I'm reading my Bible. The more I study scripture, the more questions I have. Most aren't about Christ or faith. My ponderings sound more like, "What could she be baking with sixty pounds of flour?" Each time I read, I discover more of these intriguing elements.

The Parables present even more challenges. Jesus omitted many details, and I think He did it on purpose. His open-ended scenarios leave room for imagination, and if you dare, what-ifs.

For instance Luke 13 begs us to ask the what-if. The man plants his seed; the woman works her yeast. But what if they hadn't? What if they'd put their respective seeds and yeast on a shelf?

Jesus' omission invites us to explore the what-if. Although Christ describes the beauty of planting the seeds or sifting the Kingdom of God throughout the fabric of their lives, these parables call us to ask what happens when we put the Kingdom on the shelf.

It's interesting Jesus uses seeds and yeast in His parable. Both are living organisms yet appear to be inanimate. Both possess limited viability. Seeds reach their prime in the first couple of years and, even if stored in perfect conditions, will last five max. Dry yeast is similar, though its optimum season is 2-4 years. Either way, there's a shelf-life, and if we don't respect it, the seeds and the yeast will die. They'll be useless.

My mom baked bread often during my childhood. I remember the dough sitting in the warm sun-filled cab of Daddy's truck to optimize the rising. What barely filled the bread pan became huge mounds of light airy dough, tripling in size within a few hours.

The Kingdom of God is meant for living and growing. By planting it deep within our souls, it will develop and blossom, becoming bigger and more beautiful than we can imagine. Like my mother's bread, the Kingdom will double and triple in size as we work it into our nature and make it an inseparable part of our being.

The only other alternative is putting it on the shelf. We get the Kingdom of God out on Sundays or when we see folks from church. But no matter how many times we dust off the seeds so they look good for company, if we don't plant them, they'll die. The Kingdom of God becomes stagnant, without purpose. It rots and turns into something no one wants to imitate or grab hold of.

Seeds and yeast require responsibility and a bit of work, but fortunately, once you get them started, they take off on their own. So let's plant some seeds and stir some yeast into our lives. Turn the Kingdom of God loose and watch it grow.

Titles of Nobility and Respect

Do not call anyone on earth your father,
because you have one Father, who is in heaven.
Matthew 23:9 (HCSB)

Confession time . . . ancient European royalty fascinates me. In high school I read all kinds of historical fiction set during the times of King Henry VIII and Queens Elizabeth and Victoria. You can't imagine my delight when I discovered myself a descendant of the Stewarts of Scotland.

Usually I address God as Lord in my prayers. And though totally appropriate, recently it bothered me a bit. Not a few nobles from ancient Europe boasted the proper title of lord. History reveals many who referred to those above their station with 'lord' did so out fear or self-serving ambition rather than with the respect the station deserved.

How many times do we use the titles and descriptions of God out of habit or to remind ourselves of our place rather than to truly revere the One who deserves more praise than we can imagine? I started to wonder if I should call God "Lord" with the abuse the word has endured throughout the ages, and as I prayed about it, I was reminded of the verse above.

Very seldom did God restrict the titles we give to humans. Jesus asked us to save only three, Teacher, probably for the Holy Spirit, and Master, for the Messiah. The third He asked us to set apart for the One who made us. Surprisingly, it's not a title of grandeur or majesty. When we think of this word, we'd place it far below Master and Teacher. It's so common; it's most babies' first word . . . Father.

Jesus said, "Don't call anyone on earth your father." Matthew Henry suggested the Master meant Spiritual Father because of the context, and I believe he's right. But I find it very telling that the One who can be called Omnipotent Sovereign, Creator of the Universe, Master of Nature and Most Holy Awesome Lord, specifically reserves one title for Himself . . . Father.

The One who commands the seasons and sets the stars in place wants us to know Him as Father, in the fullest and most truth-filled meaning of the word. He could have reserved any title for Himself, but He chose to be known as the One who loves us more than Himself, the One who will defend and lead us, teach and care for us.

Perhaps those words of Jesus are why the enemy works so hard to destroy the image of father. So many earthly dads fall short, some more than others. These men errantly redefine the beauty of our true Father's Holy title.

God wants us to return to the origin of the word, to understand Him as the loving Creator who gave life to all. Yahweh will always be King, Lord, Creator, Omniscient Spirit, Ruler of the Universe and more, but to those who come to Him, His greatest desire is to be a loving Parent, something many have never known. The All-Powerful Provider Ancient of Days' greatest desire is to be our true Abba, your Daddy, my Father.

Friends of Jesus

I no longer call you servants,
because a servant does not know what his master is doing.
But I call you friends,
because I have made known to you
everything I heard from my Father.
John 15:15 (NCV)

Friends of Jesus . . . many places in scripture remind us God calls us friends. Unfortunately, in my experience I've found many people don't truly know what friendship means.

It's difficult for those in management to hire friends because so many believe working for a friend means special privileges and a light workload. Paul told Timothy,

Those who have believing masters
should not be disrespectful to them because they are brothers,
but should serve them better, since those who benefit from their service
are believers and dearly loved.
1 Timothy 6:2 (HCSB)

How many do you know who serve their friends even better because they are dear to them?

Similarly, I've witnessed people bail when relationships get tense. Someone speaks a harsh word; another takes things personally, and the friendship is easily abandoned. Broken bonds can only be avoided through hard work, love, and forgiveness.

Unfortunately, the body of Christ allows itself to be influenced by the world instead of the other way around. Because we're a "friend of God" and John promises blessings for the "sons and daughters of God," it's easy to take Christ's friendship for granted.

As I share the gospel, I never want to focus on a to do list. The emphasis must be on what our Savior has already done. Our only task is to evaluate our loyalty to our best friend and explore the variety of ways we can demonstrate that loyalty.

Jesus' friendship doesn't get us out of serving. Instead it elevates our service to a place of priority; we're part of the inner circle. We are now servants whose best friend is the Master. Our every thought becomes, "What can I do today for my very best friend?"

The Rest of the Story

❦❧❦❧❦❧❦❧

[17] Therefore, if anyone is in Christ,
the new creation has come:
The old has gone, the new is here! [18] All this is from God,
who reconciled us to himself through Christ
and gave us the ministry of reconciliation:
[19] that God was reconciling the world to himself in Christ,
not counting people's sins against them.
And he has committed to us the message of reconciliation.
[20] We are therefore Christ's ambassadors,
as though God were making his appeal through us.
We implore you on Christ's behalf: Be reconciled to God.
2 Corinthians 5:17-20 (NIV)

Have you ever reached the end of a book or movie only to discover you'd just finished part one of a series? The cliffhanger, the promise of something bigger and better, kept you in suspense until the next release.

Many years ago Paul Harvey recorded a weekly radio broadcast called "The Rest of the Story." He would share a true tale about an ordinary person or incident, and then he'd tell us he'd be right back with "the rest of the story." After a commercial or three, we'd hear a heartwarming ending to bring hope and restore our faith in humanity.

I believe Second Corinthians 5 is "the rest of the story."

As a Christian, I can never be too appreciative of everything Jesus did. Can you believe he left the beauty and perfection of heaven to walk on this earth, to experience life as a human so we can know He understands us?

His death and suffering on my behalf leaves me speechless, and the resurrection is too marvelous for words. When we share the gospel, we generally tell our friends these extraordinary truths sprinkled with the message of Christ's astonishing gifts of love and forgiveness. But too often, we leave it there. We don't give them a hint there's more.

I realize the basic truth of the gospel is enough; however, it's not the end. For a long time I lived with an incomplete view of the fullness of Christianity. I had a basic understanding of forgiveness and the fundamentals of salvation. My view of the gospel was from a human perspective of forgiveness.

In a world where offering forgiveness doesn't and sometimes shouldn't mean restored friendship, forgiveness and reconciliation are not synonymous. However, in a perfect Kingdom, the two are one. Reconciliation is the most exciting part of the gospel of Jesus Christ!

You see, I'm not just forgiven. I'm more than made new. The One who created me offers full restoration. Christ calls me friend (John 15:15). The Sovereign Ruler of the Universe walks me with in the cool of the day (Genesis 3:8). His Spirit speaks to my heart. My tears of regret become laughter, my sorrow becomes joy, and Jesus invites me to dance with Him. (Jeremiah 31:13) My Savior and Redeemer, the One who paid the price for my ransom, the Father I hurt beyond measure when I wasted the treasures He gave me, anxiously waited for my return, and not only did He forgive me, He ran out to meet me, brought me back into the Garden of His Estate and gave me a huge share of the inheritance just as if I'd never left.

The Bible promises full reconciliation, but too often the sequel never gets told. So as you share the goodness of Jesus as well as His love and forgiveness, remember to tell the Rest of the Story.

The Glory of the Lord

⁵ They took the things Moses commanded
to the front of the tent of meeting,
and the entire assembly came near
and stood before the LORD.
⁶ Then Moses said,
"This is what the LORD has commanded you to do,
so that the glory of the LORD may appear to you." ...
²³ Moses and Aaron then went into the tent of meeting.
When they came out, they blessed the people;
and the glory of the LORD appeared to all the people.
²⁴ Fire came out from the presence of the LORD
and consumed the burnt offering
and the fat portions on the altar.
And when all the people saw it,
they shouted for joy and fell facedown.
Leviticus 9:5-6 & 23-24 (NIV)

Every church person I talk to wants to see God. They long to hear His voice. We'd all love to see the glory of the Lord firsthand. But few are willing to spend the kind of time the Bible talks about.

In chapters 8 and 9 of Leviticus, we find a detailed account of the day the glory of the Lord appeared in a big way. Condensed into two short chapters, we often miss how long the "assembly" stood there worshipping their Creator. If you've never watched someone slaughter an animal, you probably don't have a clue the time involved.

I remember the first time it hit me, "These people were there all day!" Even for the most experienced butcher, removing those organs, the hide and the unclean parts takes considerable time. Add the rituals and meticulous instructions Aaron and his sons had to follow, and you'll discover they had a really long day.

I've heard firsthand stories from missionaries and pastors of churches in Africa who've seen God move in marvelous ways. These faith communities experience huge miracles every time they meet. Perhaps it's because their gatherings resemble this Leviticus church.

One congregation in Africa meets in a huge open pavilion. Each week more than 500 people begin to gather early in the morning. Those who live closer arrive first, but some in their fellowship walk for hours. Worship with song and testimony continues until the pavilion fills. Then they share a meal and listen to one or two sermons. Their celebration continues until the crowd gradually dwindles, each one leaving in time to walk home before dark. They share awe-inspiring stories of healings, life transformations and the presence of God in their midst.

We desperately want to see the Almighty move in extraordinary ways, but clocks and schedules take priority. Try to remember the last time you heard of an American congregation spending all day in church. I wonder if we'd experience the glory of Jesus more often if we didn't have to rush out to meet family or take our children to some sporting event. Would we see more people healed and set free if we set aside a full day to worship instead of one hour watching the time and worrying about what we'll eat for lunch?

I'm guilty as anyone. I lead worship; and as noon draws near, the clock calls me. I respect the schedules of those who worship with me, so I try to make sure we don't run too late. But how different would it be if I just kept worshipping, and when folks needed to leave, I let them leave. Would I see the glory of the Lord in the congregation more often? Might the church experience His presence, hear His voice, and enjoy fellowship with His Spirit?

I can't guarantee my worship space will change anytime soon. I'm guessing yours is the same. However, let's both give Christ our schedules, and as we begin to carve out more time for Christ, perhaps we'll see His glory a little more often.

No More Scrubbing

⟡⟡⟡⟡⟡⟡⟡⟡⟡⟡⟡

⁹ About noon the following day as [Cornelius' servants]
were on their journey and approaching the city,
Peter went up on the roof to pray.
¹⁰ He became hungry and wanted something to eat,
and while the meal was being prepared,
he fell into a trance.
¹¹ He saw heaven opened and something like a large sheet
being let down to earth by its four corners.
¹² It contained all kinds of four-footed animals,
as well as reptiles and birds.
¹³ Then a voice told him, "Get up, Peter. Kill and eat."
¹⁴ "Surely not, Lord!" Peter replied.
"I have never eaten anything impure or unclean."
¹⁵ The voice spoke to him a second time,
"Do not call anything impure that God has made clean."
¹⁶ This happened three times,
and immediately the sheet was taken back to heaven.
Acts 10:9-16 (NIV)

Imagine how confused Peter must have been at the end of this vision. Was this God or the hunger talking? Fortunately, even before he had time to contemplate the meaning, Cornelius' men knocked on his door. The vision gave him permission to break the Jewish code and go to the Gentile's home.

I've never understood why Jews couldn't associate with Gentiles, especially one like Cornelius, dedicated to following Yahweh. I don't see any Old Testament mandate, so it must have been a rabbinic law or old custom. I suppose staying out of a Gentile's home helped keep them from becoming unclean.

But what does Peter's vision mean for you and me? Does it merely give me the freedom to eat bacon?

Prior to Christ, everyday living made a person unclean. Those charged with burial were constantly unclean, and women about half the time. Burning sacrifices used in the Water for Atonement, something God commanded priests to do, brought uncleanness. Honestly, simply living made a person unclean. Avoiding Gentiles couldn't make that much difference.

The Leviticus list of unclean acts makes me uncomfortable. Very few were within human control. And for an unclean Israelite, the sanctuary was off limits. How can that be fair? But Acts 10 changes everything.

When we read Peter's story, we focus on food and people, but what if God has more for us to learn? What if the real beauty of Acts 10 lies in the truth that Jesus' blood covers us so we're never again unclean before our heavenly Father?

Prior to Jesus, life made people unclean. Mold, illness, death, touching things and more contributed to the malady. One might think God didn't want people near Him. On the contrary, I believe God spent centuries showing humans their true state. Without help, mortals could never be holy enough to stand in the presence of God because life happens.

Israel could do nothing to stay clean. But when we allow Christ's sacrifice to cleanse us, nothing can make us unclean. Our Creator sees us through the blood of Jesus. Because we believe, He calls us clean. He says to us what He said to Peter, "Don't call anything impure that God has made clean." Peter's vision teaches us that the Cross paved our way into the Holy Sanctuary.

We stress over our mistakes and let guilt consume us when we mess up. And while pleading for forgiveness and asking the Holy Spirit to keep us from repeating our faux pas is essential, we should never believe the lie that we've fallen out of God's grace. We nullify grace when we attempt to be righteous and clean by our own strength, exactly the thing that made the Israelites unclean.

So, the next time you're having a bad day, when you feel like you've let God down more than ever before, remember Peter's vision, and praise God He calls you clean!

Nazareth or Capernaum

❧ ❧ ❧ ❧ ❧

²² All spoke well of him and were amazed
at the gracious words that came from his lips.
"Isn't this Joseph's son?" they asked.
²³ Jesus said to them, "Surely you will quote this proverb to me:
'Physician, heal yourself!' And you will tell me,
'Do here in your hometown
what we have heard that you did in Capernaum.'"
²⁴ "Truly I tell you," he continued,
"no prophet is accepted in his hometown.
²⁵ I assure you that there were many widows in Israel in Elijah's time,
when the sky was shut for three and a half years
and there was a severe famine throughout the land.
²⁶ Yet Elijah was not sent to any of them, but to a widow in Zarephath in the region of Sidon.
²⁷ And there were many in Israel with leprosy in the time of Elisha the prophet,
yet not one of them was cleansed—only Naaman the Syrian."
²⁸ All the people in the synagogue were furious when they heard this.
²⁹ They got up, drove him out of the town, and took him to the brow of the hill
on which the town was built, in order to throw him off the cliff.
Luke 4:22-29 (NIV)

Everyone in Nazareth spoke well of Him. Joseph's son impressed the townspeople with his gracious speech. At first glance Jesus appears a bit tough on His hometown. But their reactions prove He was right.

Jesus grew up among these folks. Hadn't they noticed He was

different than the rest? Perhaps. But Nazareth didn't want what made Him different, and they certainly didn't want changed lives. Looking for more than hope filled sermons, Jesus' neighbors expected flattery to inspire miracles. And when He didn't give them what they thought they deserved, they tried to throw him off a cliff.

The mindset lingers today. Folks from Nazareth say they want to know Jesus, but they're really looking for blessings without change. Is that why newcomers find churches so unattractive? If the people who call themselves the body of Christ aren't more like Christ than the rest of the world, then why bother? If we're just clamoring after miracles that don't make life more abundant, what's the point? After all, what good is a healing or deliverance if it leaves the heart bitter and the spirit discouraged?

Every day offers an opportunity to choose. Will we be like the people of Nazareth, the kind who just want Jesus for external pleasures and comfort? Or will we learn to be like Capernaum? A forty-mile walk from Jesus' hometown by land, but a mere 18-inches from head to heart in attitude adjustment.

The people of Capernaum recognized Jesus' authority; and while Jesus' eloquent speech left Nazareth somewhat impressed, Capernaum listened in amazement, taking notes and letting the message grow in their hearts. Other people noticed the change as the Capernaum crowd shared lessons they'd learned. Because they recognized Jesus as more than just a carpenter's son, greater than a mere miracle maker, the village of Capernaum witnessed deliverance and healing.

So where do you live? Do you reside in a land with contained appreciation of Jesus' wisdom or a place of amazement and awe? Is Mary's Son simply a respected member of the community or have you embraced His authority? Jesus wants to be our friend. But too often, like Nazareth, we treat Him only as friend and neglect to recognize Him as Lord.

Let me ask you again . . . where do you live? Come journey with me. I'm moving to Capernaum.

The Nazareth Principle

⌾⌾⌾⌾⌾⌾⌾⌾⌾⌾⌾⌾⌾⌾

[14] Jesus returned to Galilee in the power of the Spirit,
and news about him spread through the whole countryside.
[15] He was teaching in their synagogues, and everyone praised him.
[16] He went to Nazareth, where he had been brought up,
and on the Sabbath day
he went into the synagogue, as was his custom.

. . .

[22] All spoke well of him and were amazed at the gracious words that came from his lips.
"Isn't this Joseph's son?" they asked.
[23] Jesus said to them, "Surely . . . you will tell me, 'Do here in your hometown
what we have heard that you did in Capernaum.'"
[24] "Truly I tell you," he continued, "no prophet is accepted in his hometown.

. . .

[28] All the people in the synagogue were furious when they heard this.
[29] They got up, drove him out of the town, and took him to the brow of the hill
on which the town was built, in order to throw him off the cliff.
Luke 4:14-29 (NIV)

On those occasions you've gone out of town for business or some personal emergency, have you ever returned in the power of the Spirit? After a retreat weekend, you might come home renewed. However, our homecomings generally find us exhausted without much thought to the power of Christ.

It feels good to come home. The children shower us with hugs, and our spouse makes us feel loved. Like Jesus, though, it doesn't take long for the welcome to wear off and wearisome to settle in. It begins to sound something like, "Honey, while you were gone . . ." or "Mom, did you remember I need . . ." They wouldn't treat a stranger like that! No, a guest would continue to feel welcome for days. They wouldn't be expected to find a furnace repairman, throw in a load of laundry, and wash every dish left in the sink while they were gone.

It's because, like Jesus in His hometown, our family enjoys an almost too comfortable familiarity. We take each other for granted and place higher expectations on those we love. We know our family members capabilities, and we're confident they won't let us down. It's a daunting reality, even for Jesus.

On the other hand, while we expect the most from our family, our expectations sometimes limit them. Everyone in the small town of Nazareth knew Jesus' parents and siblings. The carpenter's son would be a carpenter. That's how the world worked. How could this man they'd known since infancy be the Christ? He'd played with their kids. Even remembering his good manners and obedient spirit as a child couldn't convince them He was a rabbi, let alone the Messiah.

Likewise, with those we're closest to, our familiarity with their faults sometimes keeps us from perceiving their progress. Until it's time to buy new clothes, we don't always notice our children getting taller.

Spiritual growth works the same way. Marks on the wall would be so handy, but the things of the Spirit don't work that way. It may be difficult to see that your spouse yells at the kids less, since he still loses his temper from time to time. And your son keeping his room clean for an entire week might go unnoticed on Saturday when you walk in and the room's been trashed. You might even miss your own growth without a journal to remind you of thoughts you had early in your Christian walk.

Unfortunately, progress that goes unseen and growth no one believes can be a hindrance to those attempting to mature or change. Jesus could only do a few miracles because of the lack of faith among those who knew Him best. Similarly, growth thrown back in your loved one's face causes it to be stunted.

It's a phenomenon I will forever call, "The Nazareth Principle." Like the natives of Nazareth, when we don't believe in a person, we limit their abilities. Our negativity possesses the power to stop progress and keep people we love from being all they can be. If we pay attention, we'll see it stifling our colleagues and congregation. It's at work in children condemned because of their parents, siblings bearing the burden of their older brother's behavior, and people who have heard those deadly words their entire life: words like can't, won't, stupid, dumb, ugly, idiot.

You and I have the power to stop and reverse the effects of the Nazareth Principle. We can give people the power to see miracles in their own lives. Phrases like, "you can do it," "I believe in you," "I love you," and most importantly, "Jesus Christ loves you and created you to be more than you can ever imagine," can recreate them. We can be that lone adult in a child's life who believes they were created for greatness. It's up to us to see the possibilities and the promise of more, to look at the potential rather than the present, and help them realize past failures, poor choices and character defects don't define their future.

Words of love, encouragement, acceptance and belief can transform a person's thinking, being, doing and living. Our job will be difficult, because we'll be tempted to focus on the too familiar. It will be easy to miss the slow but steady growth this kind of nourishment can bring. But if we're patient and have faith, not only in the one transforming, but also in the One who brings phenomenal transformation, the miracles we will witness will be amazing.

Restoration

Then they gathered around him and asked him,
"Lord, are you at this time
going to restore the kingdom to Israel?"
Acts 1:6 (NIV)

Human nature seems pretty consistent, and those closest to the Savior easily fell into the stereotype. They'd spent nearly three years walking with Jesus, eating with Him and hearing Him teach, still the eleven had only one thing on their minds. They wanted to see Israel live in the glory she had under King David. Even watching their Friend suffer on the cross hadn't changed their focus.

In their defense, all of Judea expected a conquering Messiah. Like people today, these ancient God followers probably interpreted scripture around the parts that confirmed their beliefs. The suffering servant of Isaiah 52 and 53 didn't make the cut; and they must have believed David's cry in Psalm 22 reflected his own sorrow, not the foreshadowing of a great Savior.

The whole scenario reminds me how often my prayers focus on me. I believe God wants to hear my heart, every cry and complaint. However, like the disciples, when I fixate on my little world, I miss the truth of the restoration Jesus came to bring.

For instance, if we turn the page to Acts 3, we see a lame beggar walk after Peter's famous, "Silver and gold have I none, but what I have I give to you." It's easy to celebrate Peter's ability to perform miracles; but read on. What if the healing was merely a portal for the good news of Jesus? Would the town have listened without seeing the man walk? We compartmentalize scripture with the headings and chapter divisions, but could this cause us to miss the story's beautiful ending deep in chapter four, "the number of men who believed grew to about five thousand"?

The lame man rejoiced, and so he should! What a blessing! What a wonderful story of personal restoration. And although heaven shared his excitement, his healing was a drop in the bucket. Jesus' power goes beyond Israel. Our Messiah came to restore the original Kingdom, Eden, along with every son and daughter of Eve.

God does grant individual blessings. We can't dismiss those gifts. But I also never want to be so concerned with my own little world I miss God orchestrating a million scenarios all at once to advance His glory and restore my brothers and sisters to our true home, the Kingdom of Heaven.

When Failure Haunts You

〰〰〰〰〰〰〰〰

¹² When the angel of the LORD appeared to Gideon,
he said, "The LORD is with you, mighty warrior."
¹³ "Pardon me, my lord," Gideon replied,
"but if the LORD is with us,
why has all this happened to us?
Where are all his wonders
that our ancestors told us about when they said,
'Did not the LORD bring us up out of Egypt?'
But now the LORD has abandoned us
and given us into the hand of Midian."
Judges 6:12-13 (NIV)

Had I been the angel when Gideon asked, "Why did all this happen?",
I believe my response may have been something like "We warned you this
would happen," or "What did you expect when the whole country started
following fake gods?" I want to shout, "Abandoned you? You abandoned
God!"

The Creator's list of legitimate reasons for allowing Israel to fall
grew daily, so helping them understand their part in the problem seems
reasonable. He'd even sent a prophet just a short time before to tell them, "I
told you not to worship those gods, but you didn't listen" (Judges 6:10)

But God did what God does; He ignored the question because the
answer had nothing to do with the mission. Instead Israel's Commander-in-
Chief said, "Go in the strength you have and save Israel."

No reprimand, no reminder of their mistakes, just a command to get up and get going. In this simple dialogue we see a tiny piece of God's nature, a little insight into the Sovereign King of kings.

Humans tend to be quite different. In an effort to create our own holiness, we like to use our spiritual mistakes to beat ourselves up. And unfortunately, reminding each other of our missteps keeps us equally busy. Sometimes we hope we can fix one another, as if God needs our help; and other times, if we're honest, we feel powerful when we punish each other over and over again.

Gideon's story teaches us our Heavenly Father refuses to rehash our wrongs. He wants us to learn from our mistakes, but even before we get it; God forgets it. Those thoughts that bring blame aren't the voice of the One who formed us in the womb. Rather, our enemy feeds our insecurities.

The same forgiving Spirit that spoke to Gideon inhabited Jesus when the elders brought the adulterous woman. (John 8) Our Savior didn't mention the woman's mistakes. He showed her the next step. The Almighty doesn't remind us of our failures, He simply points us to the path that will take us past them.

Looking for Joy

Christ is preached. And because of this I rejoice.
Yes, and I will continue to rejoice.
Philippians 1:18 (NIV)

The world needs joy, a fruit that's often in short supply. Some folks confuse joy and happiness. Happiness is the feeling you get when something good happens. Joy is something deep inside that stays even when happiness fades.

The words joy and rejoice occur thirteen times in the book of Philippians. That doesn't sound impressive until you consider Paul's circumstances when he told the people of Philippi, "I always pray with joy . . ." (Ph 1:4).

If we read on, we discover the words, "I am in chains for Christ." In the midst of a prison sentence, Paul writes about joy. He proves joy is not dictated by circumstance, but perspective.

Paul gave his imprisonment credit for advancing the gospel. He could have wallowed in self-pity, but instead he celebrated as the guards took notice of his faith. He rejoiced because his sentence emboldened others. The great apostle had every right to complain. He chose to focus on the good and found joy.

Paul makes it look easy, but we know better. I wish I could say I always find the wonderful, but sometimes I forget to look. Too often I focus on the negative right in front of me instead of lifting my head toward the beauty around. I forget to ask Christ to help me see the joyful moments. The masterpiece often hides behind the mess, and sometimes it's only by the power of the Holy Spirit we move away the grime to see God's greatness.

Sometimes our situations seem too bleak to find any good. When these times come, remember Paul, in prison for preaching the gospel of Christ, not knowing for certain when or if he'd ever be released, yet full of joy.

Joy like Paul's can be ours. As we search our Creator's greatness in everything and allow the Holy Spirit to show us beauty in the ashes, we'll be empowered to live life like Paul, with unexplainable joy.

No More Cracks

The light has come into the world,
and people loved darkness rather than the light
because their deeds were evil.
John 3:19 (HCSB)

Have you ever filled the grooves of old paneling with drywall mud? Seventies style walls can be transformed into something more modern without demolition and reconstruction.

I used this technique on a huge room. It took a few days to apply several thin coats of mud. After filling in every divot, we wet sanded, ensuring all the ridges were completely filled without bumps or indentations. And while this sounds like the final step, we then set a spotlight almost parallel to the wall. A flip of the switch reveals any minor flaws that remain.

Four times Jesus calls Himself "The Light of the World." John uses the phrase to describe the Savior two more times. The light illuminating my plaster faux pas showed me how Jesus does the same thing.

Most people aren't evil, not in the way we think of the word. Even before I began my walk with Christ, I don't think anyone would have used that adjective to describe me. If you had asked what I needed to change, I'd have mentioned a few missing graces to avoid looking conceited but saw little wrong. I lived a socially acceptable life. People liked me, and I tried to help others.

But then the light turned on.

When I began to walk with Jesus, He shined His brilliance on me. Like the lamp on the walls I mudded and sanded, Christ exposed flaws and mistakes I didn't know were there. His splendor unearthed things only a perfect and holy God would describe as evil. Perhaps this stops some folks in their walk with Christ. Some prefer not to see the rough edges and tiny ridges. We don't need to work on what we can't see, correct? Won't that make life easier?

Unfortunately easier is not necessarily better.

Jesus wants us to have the best life possible. He came to give abundant life. But this comes when we walk in His light. 1 John 1:7 says,

> *If we walk in the light as Jesus is in the light . . .*
> *His blood purifies us from all sin.*

Jesus came to get rid of the chips, gaps, and protrusions. Sometimes the purification process scares us because human nature prefers easy. But I don't want easy, I want better!

So I pray today you are walking in the Light, letting Him unveil every ridge, crack, and bump; so Jesus Christ can finish you to perfection, and you can live the most abundant life possible!

Life in a Foreign Country

For this world is not our permanent home;
we are looking forward to a home yet to come.
Hebrews 13:14 (NLT)

Jesus said, "My kingdom is not of this world.
John 18:36 (NIV)

As it is, you do not belong to the world,
but I have chosen you out of the world.
John 15:19 (NIV)

The last full-time job I had kept me on as a temp. For the past ten years I've covered for vacations and illnesses and lent a hand during busy times. Recently, I covered a vacancy. This meant showing up every day, nine to five, leaving early a couple days each week to help with the youth and work with the praise team.

After two months I caught myself falling into an old habit. I tend to pour myself into everything. I don't like to let people down or do things halfway. In my weekly planning I nearly shuffled my church schedule so I could be more helpful at work. And God spoke to me, "That's not your job."

I could justify my zeal because doing my best brings glory to my Heavenly Father. The fine line between glorifying God and glorifying myself blurs easily. So while I continued to give my all during the hours I clocked in, I knew I couldn't allow the temporary employment to get in the way of my primary obligations.

"This job is not my job," reminded me of the phrase, "This world is not my home." Though not a direct Bible quote, it's a theme that runs through the New Testament, and everyone who puts their trust in Christ eventually begins to understand first-hand what it means.

It's so easy to pour ourselves into the world. We do it every day. Our family, friends and work pull us in. The line between bringing Jesus to the world and letting the world entice us gets fuzzy.

I think that's why the conversation from John 15 includes Christ's mandate, "I am the vine . . . remain in me." Prayer, Bible study, and fellowship keep us connected to Jesus. When we stay in contact with Him, we know what's going on in our home country. Peter tells us we should act like aliens and strangers while we walk on this planet, but this temporary assignment feels pretty comfy sometimes.

So as we journey through this strange land, we mustn't forget where we come from. Let's make plans and carry out the tasks of our homeland. Because this job is not our job and this world is not our home.

The Last Snowfall

ᖖᖙᖂᖙᖂᖙᖂᖙᖂᖙᖂᖙᖂᖙᖙ

For we are his workmanship,
created in Christ Jesus for good works,
which God prepared beforehand,
that we should walk in them.
Ephesians 2:10 (NIV)

You saw me before I was born.
Every day of my life was recorded in your book.
Every moment was laid out
before a single day had passed.
Psalm 139:16 (NIV)

I truly love snow, though I wish it came without the cold and dangerous driving. Like most of the northern population, I tend to complain even though I know I should focus on the beauty.

The uniqueness of snowflakes amazes me. Gazillions of crystals fall every winter, no two alike. It's a puzzling phenomenon. With only six branches, you'd think the odds of finding matching flakes would be good. However, each arm grows a variety of smaller stems creating a diverse collection of one-of-a-kind frozen droplets. Not even Wilson Bentley, the farmer who collected and examined 5,000 snowflakes found a pair of twins. The Creator engineered them so the process could never reproduce itself, and He fashioned humans in much the same way.

I find DNA as mysterious as snowflakes. Prior to its discovery, no one completely understood each human's complex uniqueness. Identical twins swabbed in exactly the same location never share more than 99.99% DNA. Their fingers leave exclusive imprints, and the each usually possess one other identifying marker so small only their mother will spot it.

We are God's workmanship. Like snowflakes, we may discover small motifs in humans that match, but we'll never find two altogether the same. The many talents and gifts, impediments and differences demonstrate the Maker's ability to weave together limitless beauty.

How much better would the world be if we began to look at each other like snowflakes, uniquely created, handcrafted, by the Master Designer? And what if we started looking at ourselves in the same way? What if I quit comparing myself to my friend? What if we encouraged children to embrace their uniqueness in Christ instead of trying to fit in? How many fall into sin trying to conform or rebelling because they feel like they don't belong?

You might live in a place with no snow; still each day offers an opportunity to appreciate the unique beauty of creation. Not just in the flowers and the trees, but in every human we meet. I pray we learn to see and treat others as Christ does, hand-fashioned in the Father's image; just waiting to be saved by the blood of the Son and transformed into their true unique character by the power of the Holy Spirit.

Holding Your Hand

23 [Lord], I am always with You,
You hold me by my right hand…
25 Earth has nothing I desire besides you.
26 My flesh and my heart may fail;
but God is the strength of my heart.
Psalm 73:23-26 (NIV)

Many years ago our family took a trip to the Columbus Zoo. Our ten-year-old walked beside us most of the day, while the youngest rode in a Red Radio Flyer wagon. Sylvia held Daddy's hand.

Near the end of our fun, Steve stopped abruptly. With a panicked look on his face, he said, "Where is Sylvia?" My mother, brother and I stared at him like he'd grown an extra head. Again he asked the question in an even more frantic tone, yet we stood there perplexed. Steve grew angry at our expression, and every passing second only made it worse. His demeanor quickly changed when a four-year-old said with a little tug, "Here I am, Daddy, I'm holding your hand."

Decades later, we still laugh when we look through pictures or reminisce about the day. The plight of the priest who wrote Psalm 73 reminded me of our zoo trip.

So often, like the Psalmist and Steve, we focus on things around us and forget who holds our hand. We see evil prosper and cheaters win. Someone else gets the promotion, and life deals trouble to those who don't deserve it. It's easy to wonder, "Why did God let go of my hand?"

Steve had walked all day. He carried our four-year-old more than once, and the crowds made it easy to lose track of one another. In much the same way, our routine wears us out. Life gets heavy, and we lose sight of the One who walks beside us.

The Psalmist encourages us to enter the sanctuary of our Heavenly Father. Whether it's a physical building or a time we set aside to be refreshed by His Spirit, we need sanctuary, a place of rest and freedom. Inside the quiet place, the Psalmist felt God's tug and noticed his Beloved still held his hand. Those moments spent with Christ draw us back into the truth. They remind us of realities we might not otherwise see. God is our strength, and nothing on earth can fulfill our desires. Our Savior walks by our side, and even when we aren't aware, He always holds our hand.

The Day when God did Nothing

26 Then he released Barabbas to them.
But he had Jesus flogged, and handed him over to be crucified.
27 Then the governor's soldiers ... stripped him and put a scarlet robe on him,
29 and then twisted together a crown of thorns and set it on his head. ...
30 They spit on him, and took the staff and struck him on the head ...
Then they led him away to crucify him.

. . .

45 From noon until three in the afternoon darkness came over all the land.

. . .

50 And when Jesus had cried out again in a loud voice, he gave up his spirit.
51 At that moment the curtain of the temple was torn in two from top to bottom.
The earth shook, the rocks split.
Matthew 27:26-51 (NIV)

In the late 80's our middle daughter had what we believed to be the flu. But she soon developed a fever. No amount of tepid baths and Tylenol would keep it down. Despite the high fever, the hospital staff merely put her in cool water, then sent her home with a pale face, sunken eyes, and three days worth of antibiotics. They had no idea if the medicine would help.

Now, I realize in today's culture antibiotics can work in three days, but in 1989 Z-Paks didn't exist. Amoxicillin always required a ten day regimen. So, after a day or so of antibiotics, with the weekend coming and the knowledge that three days of this drug was not going to do the trick, we called our family doctor. He immediately sent her to Akron Children's Hospital because he believed she had spinal meningitis.

Diagnosing meningitis requires a spinal tap. The doctors inset a long needle near the base of the spinal column and drain fluid to see if it's infected. It's such a painful procedure the doctors asked us to stay outside the room because it's easier on everyone.

Standing near the door, I kept listening for sounds of a child in pain. However by this time, our wee one didn't have the strength to cry. As I stood there, holding back my own tears, I prayed. I prayed for myself, my little girl and the doctors. And as I prayed I thought about God on the day His baby hung on the cross. The thought God knew exactly how I felt comforted me.

Powerless, I wanted to rush in and rip her out of that room. I could only imagine the agonizing pain she felt. Every instinct told me to rescue her. As I felt the anguish that perhaps only a parent can feel, I began to realize in a new way just how much my Heavenly Father must love me.

I let my precious little girl suffer because she needed the test to get better. But could I have let her suffer that kind of pain, and worse, for the sake of others? If her suffering on that day had only been so someone else could live, I'm not sure I could have stood there and done nothing.

Yet that's exactly what God did. He could have stopped the torture at any time, but He chose to be silent. I wonder if the sky grew dark because our Sovereign Father couldn't bear to watch anymore. As a parent, I'm convinced His love for me was the only thing that kept the Almighty from using His omnipotence to end the torment and destroy those causing it. He knew I could never stand in His presence without His Son's sacrifice. The Creator loves me so much He allowed the heinous death of His Only Son so I could spend eternity with Him.

The Bible says the curtain in the temple ripped in two from top to bottom when Jesus breathed His last. Scholars tell us it symbolizes Christ opening the way for humans to have direct access to the Father. I picture God's righteous anger ripping that curtain and saying, "Do you see what this cost me?"

Of all of the things God has done since the creation of the world, nothing says "I Love You" as much as the crucifixion. Jesus said, "I love you" when He agreed to be the perfect sacrifice for our sins and allowed Himself to be tortured beaten, humiliated, and crucified. And His Father, my Father, said I love you on that same day, the day when God did nothing.

What Kind of Race are you Running?

You were running a good race.
Who cut in on you
to keep you from obeying the truth?
Galatians 5:7 (NIV)

My daughter is a personal trainer. She gets up every morning at 5 a.m. to work out for at least thirty minutes before her two wee ones wake. She runs a 5K about once a month, and while she always races to win, even if she doesn't come in first, whenever she beats her best time, she considers it a victory.

In addition to traditional races, she's also participated in a few "Tough Mudders." Some might call a Mudder an obstacle course. I put it more in the torture/endurance category. In a Tough Mudder, teams run a mile then face some kind of challenge. The course repeats the process about seven times. Each challenge involves some sort of upper body strength, cold water, or a "fear factor" element, like running through tiny electrically charged wires. My daughter's goal was not to finish first, but to finish with her team.

Galatians reminds me of these two very different kinds of races. When we begin our journey with Christ, we start out running a 5K, free to be the person Christ created us to be. Soon we start listening to those rule followers, and we start to stumble. When we allow humanity's rules to define our Christian walk instead of the Spirit, it's as if we've decided to take on the Tough Mudder obstacles instead of staying the course of the 5K.

Like a 5K, our race may have difficult segments. There's an annual race not far from me that includes a three-and-a-half-mile hill. Even with an incline of five-hundred-feet, runners from across the globe come to take on the challenge. Likewise, our life race may have as many demanding parts as smooth.

As we walk in the faith, it's easy to get caught up in the "shoulds," the obligations and rituals. But all those have to's steal our joy and take our freedom. They "abolish the work of Christ on the cross." If rules could bring salvation, then Jesus died in vain. It's time to run the race without the obstacles, avoiding those things that cut in and trip us. Let's walk in the Spirit and live in the freedom Christ died to give.

Running Toward the Beautiful

He makes all things beautiful in His time.
He sets eternity in the human heart;
yet no one can fathom what God
has done from beginning to end.
Ecclesiastes 3:11

Spring came early this year. Or so we thought. Even the birds and trees anticipated an early thaw. Finches began singing their spring songs at the end of January, and a flock of robins littered my lawn on Groundhog Day. The leaves know it's not time; still they insist on peeking out in the warmth. We felt certain we'd gotten off easy this year.

Today, in mid-March, the heavy white covering on the trees lingered well into mid-morning. More than a thick frost, yet not quite snow, those ice crystals sent the maple tree buds back into the branches and silenced the song of the sparrow. Nature demonstrated the folly of running ahead of the Creator.

Too often, I fall into the same pit as the songbirds. I see a small opening and assume I know God's plan. With confidence I forge ahead, positive I see the path my Father cleared. It's not long before I'm picking myself up from stumbling or climbing out of the hole I didn't see. Then I remember. My Savior said to follow.

Many times God gives glimpses into the beauty He's creating to give us hope. Unfortunately, those peeks at His perfection sometimes inspire us to run ahead when He really means for us to wait. It's not a new phenomenon. God took twenty-five years to fulfill His promise of a son for Abraham, and

Sarah's lack of patience produced Ishmael as a demonstration of the problems that come when we run ahead.

Like the robins, I'm impatient. Waiting is not my forte. I see the possibilities, and I jump. Fortunately I've learned many lessons from my impulsiveness. I know I need to pray more and move less. My errors emphasize the urgency of being still (Psalm 46:10).

The Almighty created me with a sense of eternity, I inherently know there's more. So I reach for the moon before God finishes the bridge to get there. Nature shows me my limitations. While the Creator views time from every vantage point, I see through a narrow window. I praise Him it's a portal He wants to lead me through. And when I wait to follow Him, it's a passageway into the beauty and wonder of God's unpredictable, yet perfect, timing.

Are You Wrestling with God?

~~~~~~~~~~~~~~~~~~~~~~~~

²⁴ So Jacob was left alone,
and a man wrestled with him till daybreak …
²⁹ then he blessed Jacob there.
Genesis 32:22-32 (NIV)

Folks inside and outside of the church believe they can't question God or ask Him "why?" They've been persuaded God won't love them unless they just accept Him without reservation. Others strong in the faith, who seem to take God at face value, reinforce the misconception. Little do they know those who appear to have the strongest faith have wrestled with God on more than one occasion.

Consider the story of Jacob. When he left home, he promised his Creator that if He would take care of him and bring Him back safely, then Jehovah, the God of his fathers would be "his God." About two decades later, we find Jacob ready to cross the river on his return trip. Only a day away from the exact spot where he'd made his deal with God, he finds himself wrestling with the Almighty all night long. This story teaches us two marvelous things. We learn about bargaining with our Heavenly Father and how He feels about our wrestling with Him.

Now, don't get me wrong, I'm not an advocate of making rash deals with God. As a matter of fact, when I read the story of Jephthah in Judges 11, I'm pretty sure God rejects most deals. However, this story reveals one pact the Creator doesn't mind making. I call it Jacob's deal.

God doesn't expect us to follow Him blindly. When we say to Him, "God, I need to know you genuinely are who you say you are before I follow you with all I have," God is okay with it. He'd rather we give Him our trust because He's proven to be true than to know we'll blindly follow anything the neighbor calls a god. After all, believing the guy next door got the Israelites into a lot of trouble over the years.

And sometimes (OK, more than just sometimes) learning to trust God wholeheartedly is a struggle. Moses struggled, and David struggled. Thomas and Paul struggled. Jacob's story beautifully demonstrates how each of us comes to know the Almighty. Oh, we might discover the truth of God's word by different means, but the bottom line is, those who fully follow our Creator have all struggled a bit.

Each one of us, like Jacob, eventually comes to that place next to the river. Every time we're about to do something scary, it's like we're standing on the banks of the Jabbok. We know we have to do it, but we struggle. Anyone who seriously loves Christ, has probably wrestled at least a bit with giving up working in our own strength to follow God's bigger and better plan. And most of us, like Jacob, come away a little broken, but tremendously blessed; so blessed we don't even notice the brokenness.

If you've never wrestled or struggled with the Sovereign Lord, those of us who have want you to know it's alright. Go ahead and tell God what you think, give yourself permission to touch the Living God and see His face like Jacob did. And if you have indeed wrestled with your Heavenly Father, please be sure to tell the world. Like Jacob with his limp, show them your broken places and tell them how you've been blessed. Help others to enjoy the pleasure of wrestling with God.

Today is Just an Ordinary Day

⁴ But the priest answered David,
"I don't have any ordinary bread on hand;
however, there is some consecrated bread here—
provided the men have kept themselves from women."
⁵ The men's bodies are holy
even on missions that are not holy.
How much more so today!
1 Samuel 21:4-5 (NIV)

Some time ago a subscriber to my weekly devotions sent me an e-mail. Assuming I had an office and a secretary to take care of my correspondence, my personal response surprised him. I was flattered.

But let me come clean. Truth be told, I sit in my comfy chair every day. My husband leaves by 5:30 a.m. to drive truck, and life gets exciting when one of my grandkids comes to visit.

I love my life, despite it being very ordinary. My schedule is tremendously flexible and even more predictable. David's discussion with the priest makes me stop and consider how I view the ordinary details of my life. Do I keep myself holy even when the work is not holy? It's a question I think every Christian needs to consider.

Are my thoughts holy even when I am not reading my Bible or sitting in church? Do my actions reflect Jesus even when no one is looking? Could I eat the consecrated bread?

Our heavenly Father often repeats, "Be holy because I am holy." Obviously, it's important to our Creator that His most beloved creation live differently than the rest of the world. I don't think it means getting hung up on the rules. Being holy simply means living our lives as much like Jesus as possible. Not "holier than thou," simply holier than I used to be.

Living holy means going through life with no ordinary days, waking up every morning as though God just gave me a special gift, and walking through the day as if I have a holy and exciting mission even though I'll spend most of the next eight hours in my chair with my computer in my lap.

I'm certain I'll go back to being very ordinary some days. But I'm also confident that the more days I wake up with an attitude of holiness, the more natural holy living will become. In fact, I'm pretty sure if I keep allowing God to change me, having a holy day will soon become my ordinary day.

Reminders All Around

[Huram] erected the pillars at the portico of the temple.
The pillar to the south he named Jakin
and the one to the north Boaz.
1 Kings 7:21 (NIV)

Where I come from, we give names and personalities to inanimate objects. I called my first guitar "Sam." And while it freaks a lot of people out, it's a common practice in my culture to name all the animals, even the ones we intend to slaughter someday. My nephews have been reminded on more than one occasion to please not share the name of the family dinner with guests.

With that background you might think this verse didn't surprise me, but while we might name the cows and the ducks, every stuffed toy and even instruments, no one ever considered naming the pillars outside the church.

These weren't just arbitrary names; these names had purpose. The name Jakin means "God establishes" and Boaz means, "In Him is my strength." The International Children's Version of the Bible simply refers to the pillars by their English equivalents, giving me a feel for what it would have felt like to the Israelites as they entered the temple.

Every time they approached, those pillars would have reminded them, "In God is my strength, and He establishes me." My guitar's name did nothing to point me toward God, but all around them the Israelites placed reminders of the power, majesty, and goodness of their heavenly Father.

I know a young girl who named her dog "Paraclete." She'd heard a sermon preached on the Holy Spirit (the English translation of the Greek word Paraclete), and she liked how it rolled off the tongue. But in addition to being a fun word to say, her dog's name recalled the promise of Christ to send a comforter, a counselor, an advocate every time they called their pet. I don't think she meant to have that added blessing, but by bringing the name into her home, it couldn't be helped.

What kind of reminders do we put within our sights every day? We hang notes on the refrigerator and add events to the calendar, but do these call us to remember the goodness of God, or do they remind us of our busy lives? We have countless opportunities to help our brain focus: pictures on walls, bookmarks, screen savers, and more. Do these icons turn my thoughts toward Christ or the world with its problems and worries?

As we add new items to our home or office, post-its, dates, gifts, or tokens, let's try to name each one so it will help us focus on our Jakin Boaz, the One who establishes us and gives us strength.

God Often Speaks in a Whisper

...^{12} After the earthquake came a fire,
but the Lord was not in the fire.
And after the fire came a gentle whisper.
^{13} When Elijah heard it,
he pulled his cloak over his face
and went out and stood at the mouth of the cave.
Then a voice said to him,
"What are you doing here, Elijah?"
1 Kings 19:1-14 (NIV)

Have you ever felt like Elijah? The aging prophet had been serving God with his whole heart. Still, he felt completely alone, abandoned by everyone who claimed they knew the Creator of the Universe. Verse four reveals the heart of the prophet; perhaps the prayer will sound familiar. Elijah says, "I've had enough, LORD."

While I don't face death or persecution in my service to Jesus Christ, I still find myself feeling like Elijah from time to time, most often when I've taken on more than my Heavenly Father has asked, or scheduled too many things for the same day. I become overwhelmed. It's then I stop to pray and breathe just to survive.

When I have those days or weeks, you might even find me in tears. I'm not a crier by nature. Any other time it takes a lot to make me weepy. But on those days when I feel like I can't breathe, when the little things don't go right, I'll find myself losing it. Big mishaps generally don't get to me; it's the small things that bring me down. I know, it's crazy, but it's the truth!

During those times, God will speak to me. Like Elijah, we often have to pay attention if we want to hear Him. We look for Him in the storm and the fire, but generally He's a tap on the shoulder (check out verse 7) or a gentle whisper.

I remember one week my Provider came to me as a clear path on the road. I hate pulling out of a parking lot across multiple lanes of traffic, but twice in one of my overwhelming weeks, when I got to the intersection, it looked as though Moses had parted the Red Sea. In that same week, one of my appointments got moved without any word from me; and my very old car started even though the engine chugged hard in sixteen-degree weather. Additionally, one morning when I walked out of the house later than anticipated, what looked like thick ice was merely crystalized fluffy snow. That same day I arrived home late at night to a very steep snow-covered driveway, one I've walked up many times in the winter, yet my little car made it all the way to the top. So many simple things that could (and generally do) go wrong, fell into place.

I felt as though God whispered, "I see your need. I hear your silent cry, and I am right here watching out for you." In my younger days I may not have recognized such tiny miracles as whispers from God. Too often when things go right, especially the small stuff, I don't think much about it. That's just the way it's supposed to happen.

But as I heard God whisper in these small everyday occurrences, I wondered how often I miss the still small voice of God. How often am I too busy to hear Him or see His works? How many people would discount my story as happy coincidence or just having a good day?

I don't want to overlook those times when God eases my burden. I don't want to pass off His kindness as coincidence. And I want to make sure that I pay attention to every small thing that comes my way so I can hear God when He whispers my name.

The Beauty of Sabbath

❧❧❧❧❧❧❧❧❧

13"If you keep your feet from breaking the Sabbath
and from doing as you please on my holy day,
if you call the Sabbath a delight and the LORD's holy day honorable,
and if you honor it by not going your own way
and not doing as you please or speaking idle words,
14 then you will find your joy in the LORD,
and I will cause you to ride in triumph on the heights of the land
and to feast on the inheritance of your father Jacob."
Isaiah 58:13-14 (NIV)

Last Monday was one of the most productive days of my life! I finished my classwork, practiced for praise team, scrubbed the bathroom, did laundry, changed sheets and more! My house looked great, and I felt wonderful about myself. As I was putting the sheets back on, I wondered, "Why can't I be this productive more often?" And just that quickly I recalled my Sunday afternoon.

Several years ago, I decided to make a real effort to observe the Sabbath. Some weeks I do a great job, and others I find myself not feeling very rested or holy. But this past Sunday, I rested! I spent time with my husband and simply allowed my body to rejuvenate.

So much needs done, it's easy to forego enjoying the day and basking in the love of our Creator. Many times, even if we start to enjoy the break, we'll remember that one little thing that has to be done for Monday, and once we get started, it becomes difficult to stop.

Parents have it tougher. These small versions of themselves run around, little people who need help with homework or want extra attention. When they get a bit bigger, we may find ourselves at sporting events, competitions, or training; even skipping Sunday morning worship to get a child where he or she think they need to be.

Over the years I've learned the great gift that comes my way when I honor the Sabbath. Our Master designed us with a need for rest. In order to function as the Manufacture intended, we need seven good nights of sleep and at least one Sabbath every week. When we follow the Owner's manual and carry out the Creator's instructions, not only can we find ourselves more productive, we also have the promise of joy!

Some will ask, "What should or shouldn't I do on the Sabbath?" That's because, like Pharisees, we prefer things spelled out for us. Similar to young children, boundaries make us feel secure. But this kind of thinking binds us up in rules we end up breaking.

God gives only two directives. Don't do any work and keep the day holy. Keeping the day holy can seem a bit ambiguous if we're focused on the rules. But holy means sacred, set apart and different. We can still play games and have fun, but we'll keep in mind the things God wants rather than doing as we please. Celebrating a holy Sabbath usually means worshipping with the body of Christ and carrying to God the prayers and praises of His people. We should be rejoicing with those who rejoice and mourning with those who mourn. Keeping the Sabbath Holy is more about paying attention to and acting according to what God wants.

Doing no work seems pretty straight forward, but the Pharisees managed to abuse this one too. They made people feel guilty when they walked too far or cooked. I honestly don't think God concerns himself with an index of what is and isn't work. I have a friend who loves to ride the lawn mower. Taking care of the yard seems like labor to me, but others use it as a time of praise and worship. We don't need a list of do's and don'ts. If we simply ask our Sovereign Lord what He'd like us to do, we'll get it right every time.

I hope this short meditation gives you permission to take a Sabbath. Honor the day by doing what pleases God. Perhaps He's giving you time to play with your children or enjoy your spouse. Maybe your Heavenly Father knows you need a day to rest and relax. Read a book, take a nap, or play a game, whatever you decide, just remember, God loves you and wants the best for you. Walk with Him, especially on the Sabbath, and get ready to "ride in triumph on the heights of the land and feast on your inheritance."

The Wall of My Faith

... a flimsy wall is built, and they cover it with whitewash.
Tell those who cover it with whitewash it is going to fall.
Ezekiel 13:8-16

A few years ago, my husband and I drove past an ongoing construction project every day for weeks. They cleared the land and then began laying block for the new home.

Slowly but steadily, row by row the structure began to grow. However, when he saw the first few cinder blocks laid, my husband said, "That wall will never stand."

You see they put that first course of block right on the ground, with no foundation. When the rain fell the first time, right after the free-standing basement had all ten courses complete, the entire structure collapsed. To the untrained eye, the wall looked fine, but those who knew about construction predicted its destruction.

Tragically, all across America, and perhaps throughout the entire world, flimsy walls go up every week. Some are structural and lead to the collapse of buildings and careers. But many are spiritual. These spiritually feeble walls collapse under the strain of life. Some begin rebuilding immediately, while others flounder for years before they find someone who can help them put the pieces together. And every day a few give up on the process altogether and never reach their full potential in life.

You see, spiritual walls need a good foundation. But so many try to build on good works, rules, and rituals. Some use self-help books, motivational speeches and world values to start the construction. These lives look beautiful, like the whitewashed walls of Ezekiel's time, but when the first strong storm comes, the building begin to tumble. Some withstand the first few torrents, but eventually, without the foundational bedrock of salvation in Jesus Christ, those spiritual walls cave in, and many will never rebuild.

It's not just an Old Testament concept, in 1 Corinthians 3, Paul dealt with the matter, too. He said some Christian leaders were building with sticks and straw, materials that would burn when they went through the fire of life.

We need to regularly check our base. Is our faith built on the foundational love and knowledge of Jesus Christ, or do we try to be good enough? Do we lay strong blocks on our foundation? We can choose building tools like God's Word, Bible study, Christian fellowship, and the like. Or we can study other books and follow the wisdom of the world, ignoring God's commands and trusting in our own goodness to build your wall.

In Ezekiel's day the prophets and leaders were building flimsy walls of faith. Paul pronounced it a problem in the early days of Christianity; and today is no different.

I pray each of us will look at our lives daily. I hope we'll examine our foundation to be sure we build on nothing other than the truth of Jesus Christ. And once that foundation is solidly laid, may we use only gold, silver, and costly stones to continue the structure, not possessions of the world, but precious nuggets of God's truth.

This way when those storms Jesus predicted in Matthew 7 come, our house will stand strong and firm on the Rock of our foundation, Jesus Christ.

One Brick at a Time

... You are like whitewashed tombs,
which look beautiful on the outside
but on the inside are full of the bones of the dead
and everything unclean...
Matthew 23:27-28 (NIV)

As a child I loved spending summer days at my grandmother's. Grandma lived with Lupus on a very meager income, so, although I didn't realize it at the time, our fun always required very little energy and even less money. One of my favorite activities involved painting Grandma's house. Over and over all summer long, my brother and sister and I would paint the house, and we enjoyed every minute of it.

Grandma's house had a fake blond brick exterior. With a small pail of water and a paintbrush, we coated each brick. One brick at a time we changed their color, making sure every spot had the new hue. Of course, by the time we had painted half a dozen, the warm air had dried the first brick and restored its original blond color, but we didn't mind. It simply meant the game never ended.

Matthew reminded me of my long-forgotten game. Those bricks finding temporary new color reminds me of the many short-term commitments people make to Christ. Some say they want to grow in Christ, but don't do anything about it. Church attendance doesn't change. Bible reading doesn't increase. There's no small group attendance. Giving stays the same.

In my childhood game our fun cleaned the bricks and changed them for a short time, but the heat of the day and a light breeze erased our hard work.

Committing to Christ with no desire to change produces similar results. We may clean-up our act for a while, but until we allow the Holy Spirit to genuinely work within us and make a decision to change, the winds of this world and the fire of trial will dry us up, returning us to the state we thought we'd left forever.

Jesus compared that lifestyle to whitewashed tombs. Folks in His day tried to make the stone sepulchers look better, but no amount of paint could change the fact dead bones lay inside.

Christ wants us to have a full life, overflowing with love, joy, peace, patience, kindness, faithfulness and more. We . . . no, wait . . . let me rephrase that, YOU are His passion.

However, in order to reach the heights our Creator planned for us, our commitments have to come from the heart, not just the mouth. Our actions must mirror our words. When God sees our small efforts to improve, He steps in and starts to authentically change us. Not just cleaning us up on the outside but replacing the dirt and deterioration with beauty and abundance, making us new, one brick at a time.

The Next Big Thing

⚬⚮⚮⚮⚮⚮⚮⚮⚮⚮⚮⚮⚮⚮⚮

Well done, good and faithful servant!
You have been faithful with a few things;
I will put you in charge of many things
Matthew 25:14-30 (NIV)

I don't like to exercise, but I sit a lot, so I really need to do something to burn calories and get my heart pumping. To that end, when we moved in 2012, I decided I would walk as often as possible. The new neighborhood makes for a great walking trail. With minimal traffic, the paved streets include several inclines that make it a pretty good workout.

During my first two outings, I took the most obvious path. Just a little under a mile, it boasts three relatively steep hills, so I can get about twenty minutes of cardio right outside my front door.

The third time out, I had only walked about 200 yards, when I came to the "Y" in the road. As you might guess, it's not a new "Y". This, however, was the first time I had considered leaving my neighborhood. This new path leads to the neighborhood just behind my cozy comfort zone. I had no idea how far I'd have to walk to get there or the lay of the terrain. A sharp turn just beyond the "Y" hides any houses or answers.

For several seconds I weighed the options. I was tired. I'd gotten up early that morning, and it had been a long day. I knew the familiar path would take twenty minutes. This new path was completely unknown. But somewhere deep within, I felt God telling me to take the new route.

Since God spoke to me, you might think I immediately changed my direction and embraced the new road; however, my Creator's voice only changed the way I contemplated. Now, instead of weighing pros and cons, I began praying, "Lord, do you honestly want me to take this path?" "I'm tired, and I'd like to just get done." "Why do I need to go this way? Is it truly you leading me on this road? There's a lot of gravel right here. I could slide, and I don't even know what's around that turn up there."

I wish I could tell you God whispered a wonderfully profound answer, but, "Will you just obey me?" was all I heard.

By this time, you're thinking, "Now I know she turned toward the new neighborhood." I am tremendously grateful you have such faith in me; however, I thought instead, "Are you sure, God?"

I did not get a definite verbal answer, but deep inside I sensed that if I truly wanted to be called a servant of the Most High and Sovereign Creator of the Universe, I had to take the path less traveled. It only sees a few cars each day.

The new path ended up being about a mile and a quarter. I walked to the dead end and returned home completely exhausted fifty minutes later.

As I walked, I considered the times God asks us to do things just to see if we're paying attention, to give us an opportunity to practice being obedient so that when the big things come along we'll be prepared, we'll know His voice, and we'll be quick to follow.

We normally associate the Parable of the Talents from Matthew 25 with the way we spend money or how we use our talents. I think it can also help us understand God's perspective on obedience. The master gave three servants the same small task, "Take care of this money while I'm gone." The first two not only followed directions, they went above and beyond, and received the master's praise, "Well done, good and faithful servant. You have been faithful with a few things; I'll put you in charge of many things."

When God asks us to do something, no matter how small, He expects us to carry it out. Not in our own way or in our own timing; that's what the third servant did.

God will sometimes ask us to carry out the simplest of directions in a way that honors Him so we'll be ready, totally prepared, for that moment when He says to us, "You've been faithful with these small things, check out this next big thing."

Great Expectations

Humans love science and math. You might think you don't, but honestly, everyone does! The predictability makes us comfortable. We like it that experiments and equations always have the same results. Admit it, you enjoy the fact that every single time you heat an egg it becomes a wonderful breakfast food. This predictable phenomenon and others like it bring order to our day.

Unfortunately, life in general is not so calculable. Just when we think we might have it figured out, life throws a wrench in the mix. Where did we get the idea we should be able to anticipate life's next move? The Bible doesn't promise a forecastable future.

Abraham didn't know where his journey would lead; and becoming a father at one hundred had to be a bit of a surprise. Jonah certainly didn't expect a big fish, and only Samuel believed David would be king. A muddy well ruined Jeremiah's day, and when he denied his best friend three times in one evening, Peter was as shocked as anyone.

My life is unpredictable and out of my control. For some that phrase strikes terror, but I find contentment in its midst. I think much of my contentment stems from my lack of expectations.

Jesus said, "Don't worry about your life. Life is more than food and what you will wear." Then He answered the question "What do I do then?"

Our Savior said,

"Just seek me and my Father.
Look for us in everything.
Try to find the way to know us more.
When you do that, everything you need,
all of the most important things
to survive on this earth will be handed to you."

That is, of course, my very loose paraphrase of Matthew 6:33 and Luke 12:31, however, it's one of the greatest truths in scripture.

I've found contentment in life because I've learned to expect nothing from it. In those times when I invariably do, I nearly always come away disappointed. Life brings disappointment. This earth will let me down and steal my hope and joy. Every time I think I know what's coming, every time I start expecting something from life, I'm thrown a curve; and if I allow it, it will bring huge depression.

Alternately, when I "seek first the kingdom of God," life brings joyful surprises. I expect nothing, yet blessings seem to fall on me. The world might not categorize them as such. Often it's just the joy of having my whole family in the house at one time.

I believe Jesus' words to "seek first" give us a sneak peek at the secret to the abundant life Christ promised in John 10:10. Living every moment of life without worrying about the future or what my life will become has given me more freedom than I ever imagined possible. And I've discovered that seeking Christ leads to spending more time in His love and His Word. And as I learn to wait on Him, His promise of "all those things" and the feeling of supreme blessedness overwhelm me!

The Right Place at the Right Time

❧⬧❧⬧❧⬧❧

²⁶ Now an angel of the Lord said to Philip, "Go south to the road—the desert road
—that goes down from Jerusalem to Gaza."
²⁷ So he started out, and on his way he met an Ethiopian eunuch,
an important official in charge of all the treasury of the queen of the Ethiopian. . . .
²⁹ The Spirit told Philip, "Go to that chariot and stay near it."
³⁰ Then Philip ran up to the chariot
and heard the man reading Isaiah the prophet. . . .
³⁵ Then Philip began with that very passage of Scripture
and told him the good news about Jesus. . . .
³⁹ When they came up out of the water, the Spirit of the Lord suddenly took Philip away,
and the eunuch did not see him again, but went on his way rejoicing.
⁴⁰ Philip, however, appeared at Azotus, preaching the gospel in all the towns.
Acts 8:26-40 (NIV)

I'm a doer and a fixer. It's hard for me to just stand by and wait. In fact, it's so bad that one summer God called me to meditate on "Be still and know that I am God" for the entire three months. God's been molding me into a "waiter" (and not the kind that delivers food to your table) for some time, and every now and then, He reminds me the importance of waiting on Him.

So many verses in the Bible talk about waiting on God. Isaiah 40:31 says that those who wait on the Lord will have their strength renewed. In Genesis, we see disastrous consequences when Sarah takes matters into her own hands. King Saul lost favor with God because he got impatient, and the Israelites at the foot of Mount Sinai created a golden calf because they grew tired of waiting for God to give Moses the commandments. Every instance of moving ahead of God proved to be a bad idea.

Why do we think God needs our help in getting His timing right? As I've already confessed, I am one of the worst offenders. Perhaps it's because I want to be sure I'm where God needs me to be. I hope I'm always at the right place at the right time, giving Him my all. And when I finally take time to be still, I discover there's too much "I" in my conversation.

Philip's story inspires me. He shows me in order to truly be where God calls me to be, I only need to be willing to be there. Philip met the Ethiopian eunuch because He heard God specifically tell him to head that way without any specifics. God didn't tell him who to look for or what to do. He just said head that way. So, Philip did! By obeying without a verbal explanation of the next step he should take, Philip ended up sharing the gospel with a man who would change the lives of many in his home country.

It's the end of Philip's story that speaks to me most. God needed Philip in Azotus. And Philip, willing to be wherever God called him to be, disappeared without warning and showed up in there. Just like that!

I worry about always being exactly where God needs me, doing what He wants me to do. But truly, I simply need to be available. If God can lift Philip from an Ethiopian's chariot and put him down 18 miles away in a small Philistine town, I'm certain He can move me from here to wherever.

It's time to start focusing on Psalm 46:10, to remind ourselves God is God. He can do anything! He's bigger than our mistakes and blunders, mightier than our bank account or schedule. We need to cultivate an expression of eagerness and an attitude of availability. Who knows, if we get it right, we might find ourselves conversing with a neighbor one minute and helping in a mission field the next!

I've Got Connections

⁖⁖⁖⁖⁖⁖⁖⁖⁖⁖⁖⁖

¹² Just as a body, though one, has many parts,
but all its parts form one body.
So it is with Christ...
²⁷ you are the body of Christ, and each one of you is a part.
1 Corinthians 12:12-27 (NIV)

Have you ever watched the hand-eye coordination of a six-month-old? As I watch my granddaughter try to pick up things and manipulate objects, I smile. She gets so frustrated. You can see she wants to be in complete control of her limbs, but sometimes it seems they have a mind of their own.

By comparison, this morning I needed to get out the door quickly. I'd slept in, so I needed to save as many steps as possible. I didn't have time to make two trips to the vehicle, so my breakfast, lunch, water, computer, and study books hung off me and filled my hands. With the truck key between my teeth, my foot took care of the door. Every limb of my body worked together to get me there on time.

As I consider the difference between my maneuvering skills and Elizabeth's, I thought about you and me being the hands and feet of Jesus. Christ calls us His body.

When you stop and think about it, it's a wonderful plan. God is the brain. He decides what His body needs to do; then He directs each part to do its individual job in order to accomplish the goal. Perhaps that's what prompted Paul to tell us to have patience with less mature Christians. It's not that they aren't connected to the head; they just haven't grown enough to understand how to process the message the brain is sending! Much like Elizabeth's hands, our less mature members want to do what the brain says, but as hard as they try, they fail more often than they succeed.

And no matter how mature we get, we'll have those moments, days or even years when our "hand-eye coordination" is off. We get distracted and miss our mark or try to do too many things at one time and forget the main message from the brain. It's like we walked out of one room and into another and can't remember why.

Similarly, every time we walk in the dark, we run the risk of damaging parts of the body. When we stub our spiritual toes, another member of our congregation is hurt. If we spiritually fall because we trip over scripture or circumstance, the wrist that we break is a beautiful spirit trying to do the will of our Creator. And I especially wonder how our Sovereign Lord must feel when, like Elizabeth, He tries to move His hands into position, and they don't go where He needs them to be. How frustrating it must be for Him!

This week as you go about your daily routine, ask yourself where you are in your Christian walk. Are you maturing and growing, strengthening your spiritual muscles so they respond to the brain? Or are you stuck in a place where you find your toes bruised and bones broken? To get the Brain's messages we read scripture and pray, worship and share God's goodness. And whatever we do, we must stay connected to the body at all costs.

Time to Declutter

Jesus, knowing that they intended
to come and make him king by force,
withdrew again to a mountain by himself.
John 6:15 (NIV)

A stack of clutter sits in the corner of my bedroom. I didn't put it there on purpose. I had plans to put a recliner in that space, a quiet place to have devotions. But little by little, a box here, a basket there, I've accumulated quite a collection.

We call our house "The Mansion on the Hill." It overlooks the entire neighborhood. Our view goes on for miles. However, our mansion's size doesn't live up to its name. At under 1000 square feet, saving anything we don't need leads to a buildup of stuff, things I need to go through, discarding a good deal of it.

Our lives get tangled up the same way. An insult here, a failure there; they pile up, and before you know it, the clutter makes life difficult to navigate. Just like in our homes, we often need to throw things away to make room for the better things Christ wants to give us.

John tells us our Savior withdrew to a place by Himself. It looks like even the Messiah needed to declutter.

Jesus loved the people in His life. Those twelve brought Him joy and offered Him fellowship He deeply desired. Yet each also brought a bit of clutter. At least once they asked Him to choose His favorite. And three sets of them brought sibling rivalry to the mix. One or two of his friends questioned His judgement, and His family wondered about His sanity.

When you consider the crowds pressing in on Him daily, and the church leaders trying to trick Him into saying the wrong thing, we can see how Jesus needed a day off, a getaway.

So, if Jesus required some time by Himself, why do we imagine we can fill every moment of our schedule with busyness and survive?

God knew humans needed space and time to take out the life trash. He set aside one day every week especially for the task. When we recognize our need for this quiet time, retreats become reminiscent of the festivals God prescribed. And those who've learned the secrets to decluttering spend time every day alone with their Creator.

Trauma and abuse bring larger pieces of rubble. Just like moving an unused stationary bicycle from the house, these bigger hurts take more time and a little help to clear out. We need downtime and sometimes the help of a counselor. As John Eldredge mentions in "Get Your Life Back," we need time to grieve our grievances.

Each piece of clutter we remove from our lives uncovers healing. Taking out the trash leaves more room for Christ's love. And much like sitting in a room that's been rid of the mess, our quiet time of decluttering can leave a sense of accomplishment and the feeling of immeasurable peace.

Tearing Down the Walls

[decorative divider]

> [14] *For he himself is our peace,*
> *who has made the two groups one*
> *and has destroyed the barrier,*
> *the dividing wall of hostility,*
> [15] *by setting aside in his flesh*
> *the law with its commands and regulations.*
> *His purpose was to create in himself*
> *one new humanity out of the two,*
> *thus making peace,*
> [16] *and in one body to reconcile both of them to God*
> *through the cross, by which he put to death their hostility.*
> *Ephesians 2:14-16 (NIV)*

If you never shared a room with a sibling, you won't understand. Those who have know sometimes a child needs to draw a line down the middle of their space, taking care to ensure things like the door, bathroom or kitchen lay on their side of the dividing line. If you thought this only existed in the movies, you missed a huge childhood growth opportunity.

Until my baby sister started school, my middle sister and I shared a huge bedroom. We love spending time together now, but several decades ago, our space would occasionally have imaginary walls guarding our individual valuables. When one or the other borrowed something without permission or we had a life-altering fight, forgotten the next day but monumental in the moment, those boundaries let the other know a line had been crossed.

That's what I pictured as I read these verses from Ephesians. Like my

Devotions Inspired by Life | 143

sister and I, the world builds walls, the offense often forgotten before the mortar dries. And while even Christians need to set boundaries, with Christ in us, the barrier should never be built by bitterness or anger.

Boundaries keep us safe; walls of hostility hold us hostage. Boundaries set limits and provide protection; enclosures of unforgiveness breed resentment and turmoil. The Bible tells us Christ came to be our peace, to set us free. Seeing the difference between boundaries and brick walls can be tricky.

I find it helpful to remember Christ puts to death the hostility. I don't have to do that myself. Through prayer, scripture and fellowship, my Savior softens my heart and shows me how to forgive. His love destroys the dividing wall, and His wisdom sets the healthy boundaries. It doesn't happen overnight, but when I give Him access to the walled in territory, He always comes through.

When God Feels Far Away

❧◦◦❧◦◦❧◦◦❧◦◦❧◦◦

⁶ My eyes will watch over them for their good,
and I will bring them back to this land.
I will build them up and not tear them down;
I will plant them and not uproot them.
⁷ I will give them a heart to know me,
that I am the LORD.
They will be my people, and I will be their God,
for they will return to me with all their heart.
Jeremiah 24:6-7 (NIV)

My grandson and I enjoy playing Mario Kart together. He holds all the gold medals on my Wii. A decade ago, I continually had to bring him back to the couch. As he turned the wheel left, his little body moved in that direction, and when he wanted to go faster, he moved closer to the screen. He often got between me and the Wii so my controller wouldn't work. We still laugh about it.

Rainbow Road gets me every time I play. The raceway runs through space. It constantly twists, and because it's not on land, it can bounce up and down. It reminds me of those times when we feel like life is out of control. We're doing our best to steer, but no matter how hard we try, our car keeps falling off the edge. We wonder why God hasn't jumped in to take care of the situation.

When God feels far away, we find it difficult to see the Light of Christ. Sometimes our Father allows us to work in the dark to help us trust Him on a deeper level. Other times the Creator may be staying silent to help us grow. But occasionally the problem has a fix only we can implement.

Like my grandson playing a video game, we often move away from the One who cares for us the most. We work so hard to steer ourselves, we get in between the One who drives and the road. We think God moved far away, but actually we're the ones who've driven off the path and run into the walls.

Every time, if we listen, we'll hear our Lord call us back. He'll put in our heart a desire to read His Word more, and we'll feel a call to prayer. That heaviness you experience could be your Friend prompting you to become more active in His body.

Whenever we feel as though God has moved to a distant country, we need to examine our day planners. What important Kingdom builder have we left out because life got too busy? Scripture tells us over and over that God will not leave us, so if God feels far away, we know who moved. But no matter how distant we become, God will keep calling. And every message He speaks will be, "Return to Me, My child, come home."

Flexing my Muscles

Knowledge puffs up while love builds up.
1 Corinthians 8:1 (NIV)

I have a son-in-law that lifts weights. He's six feet tall, and in addition to lifting, his job requires physical strength. As you might imagine, he has some pretty serious biceps. As I read that verse from First Corinthians, I pictured my 5'2" stature wearing kids inflatable water wings standing next to my son-in-law. (OK, you can quit laughing now!)

Humans need knowledge; it keeps us safe. However, knowledge alone looks much like my water wings. I could put a shirt over them and try to make people thing I have muscles, but truthfully, it's just a lot of air. And think about the last time you tried to hug a kid wearing arm floats. Those wings get in the way! Just like knowledge. Relying solely on knowledge gets in the way of sharing Christ's love.

Gaining knowledge for the sake of knowledge generally produces arrogance. For instance, I know how to change a tire. I understand every step as well as the logistics of removing the bolts and putting them back on. But since my muscles resemble water wings, I can't do it. My knowledge is useless without muscles to back it up. And if I tried to help change the tire by sharing my knowledge, I'd quickly become annoying to the one with the tire iron.

Love, on the other hand, looks like my son-in-law's muscles. He can dig, carry, and work much harder and longer than I can. When he swims, knowledge tells him when to come up for air, but his strong muscles allow him to have fun and entertain his daughters in the pool for hours after I'm finished. Likewise, love can carry others' burdens much further than those who lack spiritual muscle. And it has the perseverance to keep going long after knowledge gives up.

We need knowledge. Paul lists it as a spiritual gift. However, he makes it clear, knowledge needs the muscle of love, otherwise it becomes useless, worthless, and aggravating. So, go ahead, flex your spiritual muscles today. Build up the world with your love!

Is Anyone Blessed Because of Me?

*From the time he put him in charge of his household
and of all that he owned,
the Lord blessed the household of the Egyptian
because of Joseph.
The blessing of the Lord was on everything Potiphar had,
both in the house and in the field.*

Genesis 39:5 (NIV)

Wouldn't you love to have a friend like Joseph? His mere presence brought blessing to Potiphar's household. Just hanging out with the guy makes good things happen. Now, that's the kind of friend to have!

But even better than having that kind of friend would be being that kind of friend. As I read Joseph's story, I wondered, "Am I that kind of person? Are my church, workplace, family, and friends blessed because I am among them?" I want to be a Joseph, the kind of person that brings blessings wherever I go!

In Joseph's younger years, he had some pretty wild dreams. And even though he didn't understand them, he believed God gave them. Joseph constantly looked for the Creator in every aspect of his life.

Additionally, Joseph must have been a person of integrity. Sold as a slave, he could have been bitter, spending his time sulking. But instead, the young son of Jacob chose to be productive, quickly rising to a position of prestige as the head servant in Potiphar's house. Later, when forgotten in prison, he chose to give God credit for His ability to interpret dreams.

It would appear the key to being a blessing lies in giving God glory regardless of my circumstances and living a life of integrity even when I have every right to feel sorry for myself.

Joseph's story inspires me. His life motivates me to be the best I can be. Not only because it gives me blessings, but because it allows me to be a blessing and causes others to be blessed because of me!

The Story of Job: The Story of the World

The Book of Job

I love meeting with others to study scripture. Even when I'm leading the group, I learn so much and often hear Christ in a new way. One night as we looked at the book of Job, the group was torn. Some in the group were inspired by his story, while even more decided they didn't need to read the book again.

Most of us shared similar concerns. We don't like God giving Satan permission to attack this righteous man. And knowing he lost all his children hurts. The three would-be friends taught us what not to do when a friend goes through rough times. And God's answers to Job's questions didn't really meet our expectations.

But the thing that stopped folks in their tracks is the question I always ask when reading the Old Testament, "Where can we see Jesus in this story?" This question brings the Old Testament to life for me, and as I contemplated the book of Job, God revealed a bit of truth. In addition to the beautiful word pictures of the Almighty and the lessons we glean about faith, I see the story of salvation from the moment of creation through the resurrection of Jesus Christ.

Job unveils a beautiful foreshadowing of all Christ would come to do. Like Job, each of us enters this world with the potential for righteousness, created in the image of God. Job's character reminds us of Adam and Eve walking in the garden with their Creator, untarnished by less than holy living.

The first few chapters of the book paint a picture of the way the enemy brought ruin to the righteous, reminding us of the devastation Adam and Eve's folly brought to the world.

Those long discourses by Job and his less than encouraging friends mirror the world after the fall. Original sin forfeits our rights as sons and daughters of God and steals every ounce of joy and prosperity we may have. Human words become hollow and useless. Life is meaningless, until, like Job, we experience restoration.

From the creation of man in the image of the Righteous Father, the entrance of sin, destruction, and loss, to the promise and potential of full restoration, Job provides a profound illustration of the story of the world.

You see, no matter what we've lost because of sin, Jesus can rescue us. Regardless of the falsehoods and presumptions well-meaning people share, we have the assurance that Jesus was sent to this earth to redeem us, to restore us to perfection and righteousness.

Like Job, some things we can't get back, but Jesus wants to make our lives better than before, to give to you and I, the opportunity to find, like Job, that a life lived in faith and trust in the sovereignty of the One who gave us life can bring us the blessing of full and lovely restoration

Always Try to Make a Good Impression

God is not impressed with
the strength of your horse or with human might.
The Lord is pleased with those who respect Him,
with those who trust His love.
Psalm 147:10 (NCV)

Humans always try to make a good impression. Most of the population spends a great deal of time worrying about what everyone else thinks. Christians prefer to believe this co-dependent thinking is limited to the secular world, but I'm inclined to believe that many within the body of Christ over-estimate the opinions of humans.

Several years ago I regularly performed concerts in churches. For each concert, I rehearsed and planned. Before one such concert, I sat in the second pew waiting for them to introduce me. For some reason, I started second guessing myself, "How will the crowd like my song selection? Should I have included this or that song instead?" I kept rehashing my playlist until I finally started praying. My conversation with God started as a cry to ease my anxiety, but after a few minutes, I realized only One person deserved my concern, my Father, my Creator, my Friend.

As I turned my attention to pleasing the Almighty and remembered He had been with me throughout the preparation process, my nerves calmed, and my anxiety washed away. I began to feel an overwhelming sense of incredible peace. The knowledge I was loved rose up within me, as well as an assurance I could do nothing to diminish the outpouring of God's grace. I was left with one responsibility, to set my heart on being who He wanted me to be rather than the person I thought the congregation might want me to be.

Most of the mistakes I've made in life had their roots in trying to impress some human somewhere. Nearly every ounce of my anxiety started with worrying about another person's reaction to my efforts. It's not that I want to go to the other extreme and carelessly disregard others. God wants the best for them too!

God is not impressed with the brand of guitar I play or the amount of RAM in my computer. He doesn't care if I write a thousand best-selling books or a Grammy winning song. However, when I respect Him, love Him, trust Him, and concern myself with whether or not my actions please Him. Then he is impressed!

Prepared for the Midnight Cry

〰〰〰〰〰〰〰〰

[1]"At that time the kingdom of heaven
will be like ten virgins who took their lamps
and went out to meet the bridegroom . . .
[5] The bridegroom was a long time in coming,
and they all became drowsy and fell asleep.
[6]"At midnight the cry rang out:
'Here's the bridegroom! Come out to meet him!'
[7]"Then all the virgins woke up and trimmed their lamps.
[8] The foolish ones said to the wise,
'Give us some of your oil; our lamps are going out.'
[9]"'No,' they replied, 'there may not be enough for both us and you.
Instead, go to those who sell oil and buy some for yourselves.'
[10]"But while they were on their way to buy the oil, the bridegroom arrived.
The virgins who were ready went in with him
to the wedding banquet. And the door was shut.
Matthew 25:1-13 (NIV)

I'm tired today. It would be easy for me to lay around and do nothing. Self-employed and working from home, no one even notices when I take a day off.

Yes, today I could easily lay on the couch and watch movies all day. It's that kind of tired. I'm reminded how easily we can slip onto the spiritual sofa and watch the world go by.

In the parable of the ten virgins, Jesus said the girls fell asleep when the bridegroom took longer than anticipated. The bride had enlisted these close friends to help her prepare for the big day. And even though the groom told them it might take a while; they'd grown weary in the waiting.

The same thing happens to the church. Ever since the time of Paul, Christ's followers have expected Him to show up any day. And truthfully, we know He can! However, like the bridesmaids, many have fallen asleep on the job. We forget our primary job is to prepare the bride.

And that's what keeps me going on a day like today. I'm called to make ready the bride of Christ. I need to stay alert so the church's white gown looks immaculate. The bride should be joyful when the bridegroom arrives, not surprised.

Five of the bridesmaids ran out of oil. Our faith, like the oil, needs constant refilling. We restock our supply in scripture, prayer, and fellowship, but many neglect one or all of these, and then wonder why they burn out.

Others don't even realize they need a refill. The Bridegroom has taken too long, and they haven't noticed their waning church attendance has depleted their oil.

I want to keep my lamp of faith filled and remind the other bridesmaids to trim their wicks. While I'm called to be a light to the world, I know if the light stays too high for too long, I may burn out. It's important to consistently return to the place where my oil can be refreshed.

I pray today your oil is full and you have an extra supply on hand, because then you'll be ready when the midnight cry sounds, and the Bridegroom returns for His beloved.

Dreams

For fifteen years or more I had a recurring dream. In each one, I lived in a cozy little house. Neat and tidy with just enough space to be comfortable, friends would have called it adorable. Each night my house looked a bit different, but it always felt homey. In every dream I sensed I had lived there a long time.

The final aspect of the dream puzzled me for many years, because every time, in every house, a house I'd lived in for years, I found a closet that had managed to escape my notice. Naturally, I always opened the mysterious door.

On the other side I discovered a room bigger than my cozy house. Sunlight poured through huge windows, and the vaulted ceilings made the great room look even more spacious. On the other side of the room, doors opened into bedrooms, game rooms, and luxurious baths. More space than I could imagine lived inside my cozy house closet. I owned it all, every inch at my disposal, yet I'd never bothered to open the door.

I don't believe every dream has a meaning. I think some show what we thought about during the day, and others demonstrate our wonderful imaginations. However, after this dream showed up more than once a week for a couple of years, I started thinking maybe God was trying to tell me something.

The book of Acts originally held the name "The Acts of the Apostles." I think a more accurate description would be "The Acts of the Holy Spirit." When we read scripture, we move from the gospels to the book of Acts without much thought, but the change in the apostles between John's gospel and Acts deserves a second glance.

In the gospels, these eleven men cower and argue, they don't always agree with Jesus; and when the stakes get high, they run. Peter denied Christ, and Thomas doubted the resurrection. But after the Holy Spirit, these guys turned the world upside down. Instead of followers, they became leaders. They gave up running for guaranteed flogging and imprisonment. In the gospels, the disciples were spectators to the excitement and adventure. In Acts, they created it.

The second chapter of Acts changed everything. Jesus had promised His Spirit several times. The apostles had seen it and even experienced it on an occasion or two before the crucifixion. But I don't think they expected the power, courage, or sense of purpose the Spirit brought.

It wasn't until after I allowed the Spirit to reign in my life that the dream stopped, and only then did I see the analogy. My dream showed me my life. I lived neat and cozy, comfy and adorable. Christ was my Savior, but I kept the Holy Spirit in a closet. God showed me if I opened the door for the Spirit, I'd discover a life bigger and better than I could imagine.

God wants me to understand there's more. Even now, after living life in the Spirit, I believe the Almighty has more. God won't fit in my closet, and He's too magnificent for me to experience everything all at one time. Every day offers an opportunity to find another door with more beauty and more grace than I can dream.

Heart of a Child

At that time Jesus said, "I praise you, Father,
Lord of heaven and earth,
because you have hidden these things
from the wise and learned and revealed them to little children.
Matthew 11:25 (NIV)

"If anyone causes one of these little ones to stumble,
it would be better for them to have a large millstone
hung around their neck and to be drowned in the depths of the sea.
Matthew 18:6 (NIV)

Then people brought the children to Jesus
for him to place his hands on them and pray for them.
But the disciples rebuked them.
Jesus said, "Let the little children come to me,
and do not hinder them,
for the kingdom of heaven belongs to such as these."
Matthew 19:13-14 (NIV)

I love watching children's programs at church. You know, the ones at the end of Vacation Bible School or after a Summer Day Camp. Those kids just want to have a good time, and they love praising Jesus while doing it. They dance and sing at the top of their lungs with no agenda other than to share what they've learned.

No child joins this world with prejudice. Little ones don't even notice differences. For instance, my curly head, red-haired granddaughter made a friend at her mother's gym. Though to any adult the ethnicity differences were obvious, the four-year olds called themselves twinsies because her little friend also had a headful of ringlets.

At about five, children begin to notice differences, often causing a bit of curiosity. I remember when my middle daughter first noticed skin color. While shopping she asked why the man three feet from us was brown. I told her, "That's the way God made him." The man's face beamed, and my daughter found the answer perfectly acceptable. It didn't change her image of the man; it simply answered the question the difference aroused.

Christ calls us to come to Him with the attitude of a child, a spirit untainted by hatred and judgement. Depending on your upbringing or your experiences, it can be difficult to throw out mindsets embedded since our teens. Those abused by a man will often throw all men into a negative stereotype. And a parent's snide remarks, even in jest, can leave a bitter taste for ethnicity or economic status.

Even in the most loving of households we pick up unchildlike habits. We're taught to stand up for injustice, but often it becomes judging. Jesus told us to hate sin, yet we allow it to spill over onto the sinner.

Christ beckons us to come to him with the freedom of a child. Children don't care if others watch them dance. They don't mind the chuckles their behavior brings; they roll on the floor laughing with us. At what age do we begin to feel laughed at instead of laughed with? And for that matter, when did we move from laughing with to laughing at?

You'd think coming as a child would be easy. Children bring with them the very definition of simplicity. Yet, the longer we allow our hearts to be held captive by hatred, judgement and worrying about what others think, the more difficult it becomes to get back to a childlike love of life and laughter. It seems an impossibility.

However, with Christ all things become possible. Each moment we allow the Spirit in, our heart softens a bit. Our Savior wants to recreate us, make us new, and form a childlike spirit within us. Because the Kingdom of Heaven belongs to such as these.

What is Normal?

*Every good and perfect gift is from above,
coming down from the Father of the heavenly lights,
who does not change like shifting shadows.*
James 1:17 (NIV)

I'm sure you've heard the phrase "The New Normal." Every few years it comes into play when something big happens. I laugh when I hear it. Because, after all, what is normal?

At eight, my life's normal changed dramatically when Grandpa died. And Grandma moving into a trailer in our backyard reinvented the word shortly after. At sixteen normal meant ten to fifteen gathered around our dinner table each evening, and just a month after my eighteenth birthday motherhood became normal for me.

Nineteen moves over the next twenty-some years brought new meaning to the word each time, and two of those moves included the addition of another family member. New vocations, technology and friends all molded my normal. Like soft clay, the shape of my life changed on a regular basis.

Those who depend on life's constants for their sanity fight depression; because the only consistency we find in the day-to-day is neverending irregularity.

In the face of perpetual motion, our only hope for true normalcy becomes Jesus Christ. Our Savior does not change like the shifting sands. The Man we find in the Bible reveals the steadfast nature of the Father.

While chaos reigns in our world, and those in it chase the new normal, we who follow Jesus have hope. We understand the only true normal lies in faith in our Redeemer.

For God who has always been holy, will always be holy.
Christ who has always been righteous will always be right.
The One who has always shown mercy will always be merciful.
God who has always shown love will always love you.

The Chorus of "Always Has" by Lynne Modranski

Things I See

> ¹⁷ *Though the fig tree does not bud*
> *and there are no grapes on the vines,*
> *though the olive crop fails and the fields produce no food,*
> *though there are no sheep in the pen*
> *and no cattle in the stalls,*
> ¹⁸ *yet I will rejoice in the Lord,*
> *I will be joyful in God my Savior.*
> ¹⁹ *The Sovereign Lord is my strength;*
> *he makes my feet like the feet of a deer,*
> *he enables me to tread on the heights.*
> Habakkuk 3:17-19 (NIV)

The day began beautifully, and the forecast called for perfect wedding weather. But as my husband put the final touches on the service, we got the call; there'd been an accident. So instead of officiating at a wedding that weekend, we stood at the groom's graveside. While still reeling from the shock, just a few days later the phone rang again. This time we mourned with friends who'd lost their son in another accident. My heart ached, wrenched with sorrow. Two tragedies in one week, both boys under the age of twenty. Leaning on Jesus became more than a song, it became my survival.

Habakkuk doesn't get much notoriety, but I relate to his oracle. Murphy's law rules, and the ancient prophet doesn't understand why God allows the devastation to continue. He cries out to the Lord twice. He doesn't see his Creator at work. He can't hear the Lord's voice. Is God listening?

Everyone has those moments, days, or weeks when we feel lost or abandoned by our Savior. The sin affecting this world sometimes seems stronger than our hearts can handle. And those are the times we need those last few verses from Habakkuk.

The prophet reminds us to praise. When the world is crashing in, and you can't go on, lean on the Sovereign's strength. Habakkuk reminds us, when we can't see what God's doing, we praise God for who He is. When the things we see bring us to our knees, Paul prompts us . . .

fix your eyes not on what is seen, but on what is unseen,
since what is seen is temporary, but what is unseen is eternal.
2 Corinthians 4:18

Drink in the Rain

‿◦‿◦‿◦‿◦‿◦‿◦‿◦‿

⁷ Land that drinks in the rain often falling on it
and that produces a crop useful
to those for whom it is farmed
receives the blessing of God.
⁸ But land that produces thorns and thistles
is worthless and is in danger of being cursed.
In the end it will be burned.
Hebrews 6:7-8 (NIV)

I live in a land rich in clay. I suppose that's why the pottery business excelled here in the early 1900's. This means hot dry summers near the Ohio River produce huge cracks in the ground. The surface shrinks from the lack of water. Weeds quickly become the only vegetation. They seem to thrive on the lack of water.

This kind of ground needs light showers when the dry spell ends because the torrential rains just roll off the baked clay. Unable to drink in the liquid, the hardened surface looks just as bad after the storm as it did before.

On the other hand, when we travel less than five miles from the river, farmland spreads as far as the eye can see. In the spring when the plowing and tilling begins, we see rich soil, dark with nutrients, ready and able to drink in every drop of water God sees fit to give it.

I see these two types of ground in these verses from Hebrews. Some of us have never allowed the Word of God to till our hearts and plow the clay under, working it and bringing up fertile, life giving soil. Depending on how long our land sat neglected, it may take years of work, turning the clay many times, adding sand and topsoil to develop the rich ground God needs to produce a good crop.

Without having worked the soil of our hearts, life's dry spells harden us. Abuse, pain, and loss all add calcification when we experience them outside of God's love. Then when the Holy Spirit pours out His life-giving rain, we can't absorb it. We miss the Father's blessings because like raindrops on the dry clay, they roll right past us.

God wants us to produce a crop. He put us here to grow the Kingdom. However, He also gives us all we need to get the job done. He offers His Word as a sharp tool to prepare the soil. He gives us prophecy in the form of sermons as well as fellowship with other Christians to increase our topsoil and add rich nutrients. And His Spirit brings soft refreshing rains allowing us to drink in His presence and power so we can be useful to Him and produce a crop worthy of the Farmer.

I Have a New Car

Keep this Book of the Law always on your lips;
meditate on it day and night,
so that you may be careful
to do everything written in it.
Then you will be prosperous and successful.
Joshua 1:8

I recently bought a new car. Twenty-eight years newer than my previous model, it has a few more bells and whistles. The first day I played with the buttons until I figured out most of the gadgets; however, I couldn't get the remote start to work, and the purpose of all the lighting buttons eluded me.

After a few days of pressing buttons with no results, I decided to check the owner's manual. Sure enough, the book had everything I needed to know, plus I found details for a couple other features I didn't even know existed. It reminded me of scripture.

Humans look for ways to make life work. They want to know the secrets to prosperity and success. Yet few bother to read the owner's manual. Right there on those pages lie everything we need to know to have an abundant life. God demonstrated the way to have the best and worst relationships and offered instructions on how to defeat our enemy. Plus He laid out a map showing us the only way home, no GPS needed.

And it's not like the book is hard to find. The Bible sells more copies every year than any other. The Gideons give them away, and many places sell paperback copies for just a few dollars. Add to that the free apps for our electronic devices, and we don't really have a good excuse for not meditating on God's word day and night.

You don't have to read it all in one sitting. Just take a verse or two every day and focus. Watch for those passages that reveal messages you've never heard before and read the ones you know well as if reading them for the first time. Every instruction you need is in those pages. Read them carefully because your heavenly Father wants you to be prosperous and successful.

Index of Scripture

About the Author

Lynne Modranski is an author, inspirational speaker, and Biblical Coach who empowers Christian leaders and inspires spiritual growth helping people move from rules to relationship and dive into Christ's abundance.

Wife to Steve, a local church pastor, she is mom to Monica, Sylvia and Julia and "Hada" to Joshua and Corryn. Worship Leader and Small Groups Coordinator of Sycamore Tree Church, Lynne is first and foremost a follower of Jesus Christ. She has a passion to help others find a real relationship with the One who has given her true life, as she shows them how they can become the very best they can be in Christ Jesus!

Lynne has written several Bible Studies, e-books, devotional readings, children's curricula, plays and advent readings. Visit her website to find out more about her Spiritual growth classes and one on one Biblical coaching.

LynneModranski.com

Cover Photo by Monica Lynne Photography
www.MonicaLynnePhotography.com

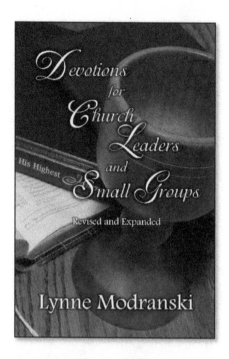

Bible Studies and Advent Readings

Curriculum for Children

52 week and 13 week curricula
available at
www.LynneModranski.com

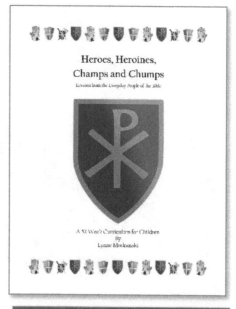

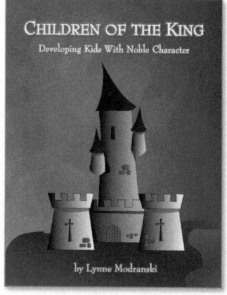

Watch for
Lessons from the life of Joseph
scheduled for release
in the fall of 2020

References

i Herms, Bernie & Gokey, Danny & Nichols, Timothy (2014) *More Than You Think I Am*. Hope in Front of Me. BMG-Chrysalis:New York.

ii Elihu Schatz, "The Weight of the Ark of the Covenant" <u>Jewish Bible Quarterly</u>, April 2007
   <https://www.questia.com/library/journal/1G1-228909311/the-weight-of-the-ark-of-the-covenant>

iii UPDATE: For those concerned I'm missing out on the good life. We now have a broadband connection as well as Netflix.

iv Taken from My Utmost for His Highest® by Oswald Chambers, edited by James Reimann, © 1992 by Oswald Chambers Publications Assn., Ltd., and used by permission of Discovery House, Grand Rapids MI 49501. All rights reserved.

CPSIA information can be obtained
at www.ICGtesting.com
Printed in the USA
LVHW010536030920
664818LV00004B/574

9 781953 374004